I Don't Care
IF WE'RE THERE YET

THE BACKSeat BoReDom BUSteR

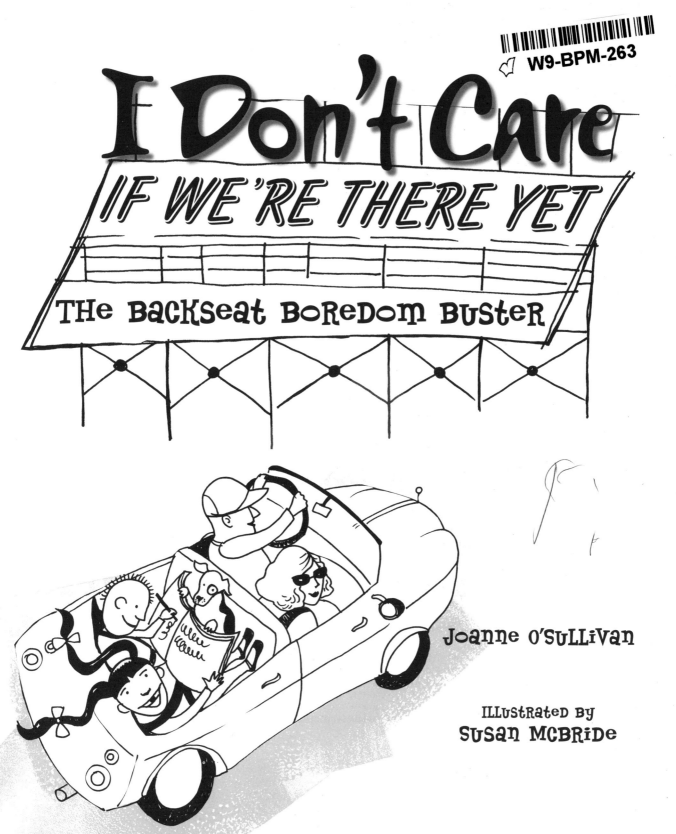

Joanne O'SuLLivan

ILLustRated By
SuSan MCBRiDe

LARK BOOKS
A Division of Sterling Publishing Co., Inc.
New York / London

Editors: Joe Rhatigan & Wolf Hoelscher

Creative Director: Celia Naranjo

Front Cover Illustration : Susan McBride

Assistant Editor: Rose McLarney

Production Assistant: Bradley Norris

10 9 8 7 6 5 4 3 2 1

First Edition

Published by Lark Books, A Division of
Sterling Publishing Co., Inc.
387 Park Avenue South, New York, NY 10016

Distributed in Canada by Sterling Publishing,
c/o Canadian Manda Group, 165 Dufferin Street
Toronto, Ontario, Canada M6K 3H6

Distributed in the United Kingdom by GMC Distribution Services,
Castle Place, 166 High Street, Lewes, East Sussex, England BN7 1XU

Distributed in Australia by Capricorn Link (Australia) Pty Ltd.,
P.O. Box 704, Windsor, NSW 2756 Australia

If you have questions or comments about this book, please contact:
Lark Books
67 Broadway
Asheville, NC 28801
828-253-0467

Manufactured in China

ISBN 13: 978-1-57990-848-5
ISBN 10: 1-57990-848-9

For information about custom editions, special sales, premium and corporate purchases, please contact Sterling Special Sales Department at 800-805-5489 or specialsales@sterlingpub.com.

For all the Dads & Moms who
make getting there part of the fun

Welcome to the Introduction

One of your adults probably handed this book to you mere moments before you and your family embarked on a vacation. Like most vacations, yours probably isn't happening around the corner from your home. You have to travel to get there. (Otherwise, it wouldn't be a vacation—it would just be going around the corner.) And, since you can't drive yet (the ride-on mower doesn't count), your adults want to make sure you keep quiet and under control while they drive. You might as well listen to them, because if you don't they'll threaten to turn the car around. (They never will.) They'll threaten to leave you at the hotel while they enjoy the rides at Disney World. (Not very likely, but we did hear about this one family...) Most menacing of all, however, is the threat of the family sing-along. (Extremely likely as soon as you whine, "Are we there yet?")

The good news is you can steer clear of countless renditions of "Home on the Range" and "All You Need is Love." In fact, all you really need to stave off boredom and horribly off-key harmonies from the front seats is the very book you hold in your hands. You see, not to toot our own horn here, but your adults made a wise choice when they picked up this book for you.

Why? Because **I Don't Care if We're There Yet** is so chock-full of utter funness (or is it funability?) that you'll actually stop caring when you finally get to where you're going! We've included hundreds of things to draw, write, figure

out, read about, fold, play, and discuss. No traditional crosswords or word search puzzles here. Also, no boring license plate games. (Ours are fun—we promise.)

All you need is a pencil. Or a pen. Markers, if you have them. That's it! No assembly required. If this book needed batteries, they would have been included.

I Don't Care... can also keep your siblings from annoying your parents. There are games to play, questions to answer, and much, much more to do with others.

Why did we do all this for you? Because we believe vacation fun should begin as soon as the last bike is on the rack and the final suitcase is heaved on top of the car. You don't have to wait hundreds (thousands?) of miles. And, anyway, what's the alternative? How about another round of "She'll be Comin' 'Round the Mountain?"

Didn't think so.

This book is also great for:
- Airports and airplanes (meets all federal regulations)
- Dentist's office (helps you ignore the drilling in the other room)
- School bus
- Aunt Lucy's house (or whichever relative keeps the thermostat at 85 degrees and offers you those hard candies that you're afraid are poisoned)
- When you're bored at home
- And any time you're waiting for something, someone, anything....

What are you waiting for? Turn to any page, any page at all. By the way, we've left you plenty of blank pages at the end for you to use to doodle, continue games, whatever.

Have a blast and send us a postcard when you get there.

Gnome Away From Home

For centuries, gnomes have been confined within the borders of forests and gardens. While these magical creatures are happy in their native environment, there lies within every gnome the urge to break free, see the world, and have big adventures. And despite their limited experience, you might be surprised by what wonderful travel partners gnomes can make. Why not take a gnome with you on your travels? Don't have one? Draw one on the opposite page and cut or tear him out. When you visit an interesting place and get your picture taken, make sure your gnome is in the picture, too. You can even write a travel journal for him—gnomes like that.

What's his/her name? _____

What are his/her likes and dislikes? _____

Write an entry in your gnome's travel journal here. _____

_____

_____

_____

_____

_____

_____

No Gnome? No Problem!

If you find yourself "gnome-less" while traveling, never fear. Many gnomeless people find substitute travel partners. Your travel buddy could be a toy or a stuffed animal. The important thing is to take pictures of it while you're traveling so that its friends back home will get to see all the crazy adventures it had.

Draw your gnome on the next page, then cut or tear him out.

The Legend of the Traveling Gnome

No one knows exactly when gnomes started traveling, but some people point to the Garden Gnome Liberation Front, a group that formed in France in the early 1990s. It is said that members of this group "liberated" a gnome from his owner's garden, and then periodically sent the owner picture postcards of the gnome visiting places all over the world. When the gnome had finally had his fill of travel, the liberators brought him home. It is now estimated that tens of thousands of gnomes travel around the globe each year. Many of them keep online travel logs of their expeditions. Some gnomes even have tracking numbers that help you follow their journeys. If you want to connect your gnome to other like-minded traveling gnomes, ask a parent if you can do an Internet search when you get home. Use the terms "gnome travel," "traveling gnome," or "gnome prank."

Boxer

Just try to stop yourself from playing this game again and again. We're so sure you'll get hooked on it that we've included enough dots for eight games. (See the next two pages.) All you need is a pen, pencil, or marker and two players.

Here's how to play:

• The goal is to create boxes in the grid by connecting the dots with lines.

• The first player makes a line connecting two dots. Play can start between any two dots on the board. The line can go up and down, or right to left.

• Now it's the next player's turn to connect two more dots.

• The first person to complete a box puts his initial in the box. If both players have the same initial, a different color or different types of writing instruments (such as a pen and pencil) could be used to tell them apart.

• Play continues until it's no longer possible to create more boxes on the board. Whoever has the most boxed initials wins.

Little sample game

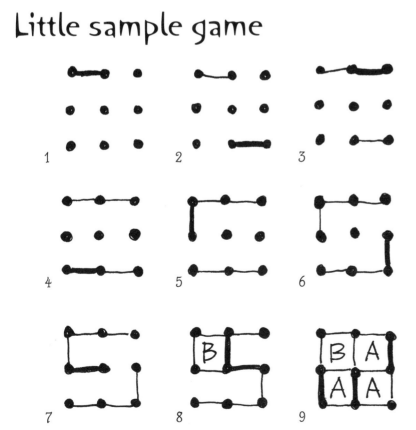

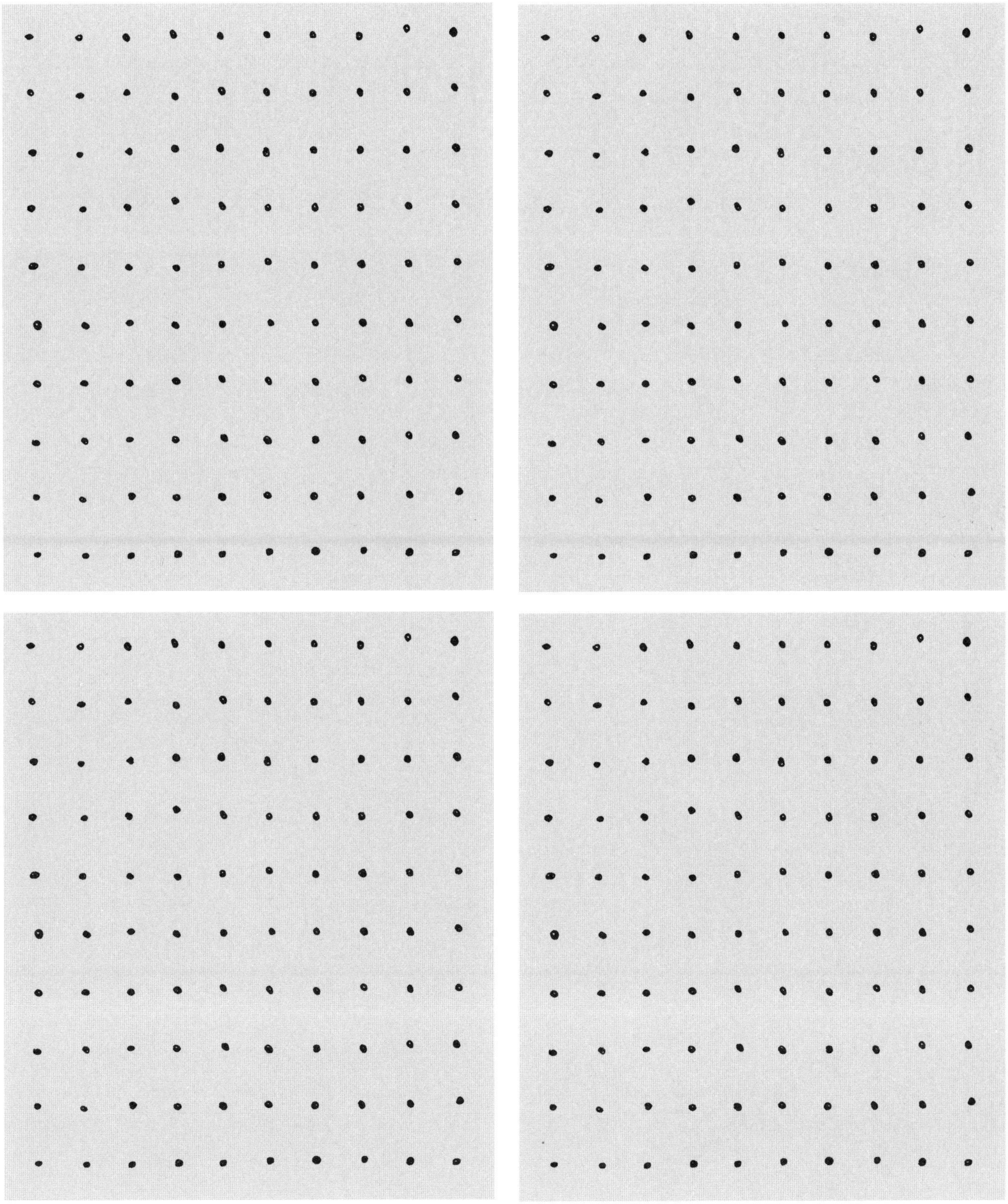

My Travel Autographs

Bon Voyage!

Your flight attendant, your pilot, that kid you played volleyball with at the beach...
you meet a lot of interesting people in your travels. An autograph is a great way to
remember them. Ask some of your travel VIPs to sign your book on these pages, so
that long after you're home, you'll still remember them.

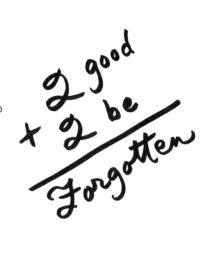

That was the best pizza ever, can
I have your autograph?   Naturally!

WELCOME

Genetically Altered Zoo

What do these creatures look like?
Draw a picture of these beasts:

- A crocoduck
- An ant-lion
- A unipus
- A gorillemur (gorilla/lemur)
- A platyroo (platypus/kangaroo)
- A moosepig
- A peafox (peacock/fox)
- A spidelephant

Or, make up your own creatures to fill your zoo.

Create more mutants!

These beasts escaped from their pens. Can you identify them?

All Thumbs

Having opposable thumbs is a wonderful thing. It's one of those great features of the human anatomy that makes it possible for us to use tools, utensils, and, oh yes, play fun games. In fact, your thumbs are all you need to play these games.

Thumb Wrestling

Ready to rumble? Here's how you start:

- Hook the four fingers of your hand with your opponent's hand so that they're tightly clasped. Press your thumb pads together in an upright position, but don't start pushing yet.

- Do a countdown to make sure that you both start wrestling at the same time.

- At the end of the countdown, each player tries to get her thumb on top of the opponent's thumb to press it down for three seconds and win the match.

Pro Thumb Wrestling

- If you want to make your thumb-wrestling matches a little more competitive, turn your thumbs into pro-wrestling characters. Draw a face (preferably a mean-looking one) or a mask on your thumb in smear-resistant ink. Give your thumb wrestler a character name. (See the list for ideas.)

Pro Thumb Wrestler Names
The Bulldozer
Kid Thumb
Krusher
Super Thumb
Captain Thumbo
Tom Thumb
The Thumper
The Mean Thumb

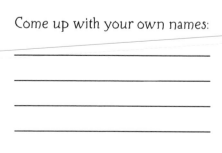

Come up with your own names:

_____

_____

_____

_____

Thumbs Up!

This game is not unlike "Rock, Paper, Scissors." First, a leader is chosen. Each player puts both fists, clenched tightly, out in front of her and decides how many thumbs (zero, one, or two), she will display when the game starts. The leader starts a count: one, two... But instead of saying three, he guesses how many thumbs, total, will be put out. If he is correct, he gets to put one hand behind his back. If he's wrong, the role of leader is passed to the next person. The goal is to get both of your hands behind your back. One last rule: if the leader guesses zero and is correct, he automatically wins.

Thumb Twiddling

"Don't just sit there twiddling your thumbs!" You might have heard this expression before, from someone who thought you should have been doing something when it appeared as though you were doing nothing. But if you are twiddling your thumbs, you're actually doing something—wouldn't you agree? Despite its bad reputation, thumb twiddling is a useful exercise in fine motor skill coordination and dexterity. And there's no better time to practice it than when you're on a long, uneventful journey. Here's how you do it:

- Bring your hands together and clasp your fingers, leaving your thumbs free. Begin rotating your thumbs around each other in a circle, trying not to let them touch. Many people can't do this without letting the thumbs touch.

- Now, try twiddling. Rotate your thumbs in the opposite direction.

- Now, see how fast you can twiddle!

- If you really want a challenge, try "pairs twiddling." Join one of your hands with another person's. See if you can twiddle without bumping into the other person's thumb.

The Thumb Game

This game is best played when you're stopped for a meal break. This way, the players might be somewhat distracted by other activities and often forget they're playing the game. One player is selected to be the thumb master. At a moment of his choosing, he will discreetly place his thumb on the edge of the table (or in another position agreed upon by all players). The other players must notice that this has been done and put their thumbs in the same position without calling attention to themselves. The last person to notice must do a silly thing at the command of the original thumb master.

Penguins & Cows

Fill these pages with as many penguins and cows as you can possibly draw.
Why? Because.

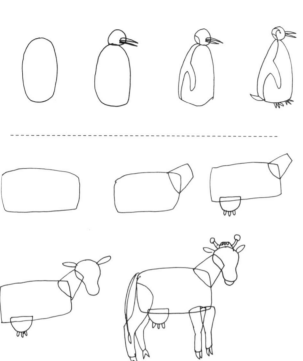

Road Trip Scavenger Hunt

Forget counting numbers on license plates—why not keep your eye out for things that are **really** interesting? Have you ever seen a school bus graveyard, the place old school buses go to die? How about a car that's older than you? Or a rock star's tour bus?

Keep an eye on the grass on the side of the road as you pass by. Can you see any UFAs (Unidentified Furry Animals)? Riding in a car and looking out the window doesn't have to be boring. You just have to know what to look for.

❑ A Building Shaped Like Something Other Than a Building
(a donut, a bottle of milk, a wagon, a hot dog)
Describe: _____

❑ A School Bus/Car Graveyard

❑ A Local Produce Stand

❑ Signs of a Recent Storm (downed trees or power lines, broken branches, smashed roofs)
Describe: _____

❑ A Historical Marker

❑ A Car Going Waaaay Too Fast

❑ A Water Tower Shaped Like Something Else (golf ball, peach, orange, tomato)
Describe: _____

❑ A Truck Convoy

❑ A Herd of Animals
Describe: _____

❑ An Abandoned Railroad Trestle or Track

❑ A Motorcycle Club (a group of people on motorcycles traveling together in a pack)

❑ A Car Built Before You Were Born

❑ A Hybrid Car

❑ A Limo

❑ A Misspelling on a Sign
Describe: _____

❑ A Sign Claiming a Business Has Something World-Famous
Describe: _____

❑ Part of a Blown-Out Tire

❏ An Abandoned Vehicle
What do you think happened to it?

_____

❏ A Truck Full of Chickens (or other animals)
❏ A Super-Deluxe RV
Describe: _____

❏ A Roadside Giant (ordinary thing made much larger than usual to attract attention: giant lobster
on a seafood restaurant, a giant flag, a giant piece of fruit or vegetable, a giant person)
Describe: _____

❏ A Hidden Police Car (Be sure to let your driver know if he/she is going too fast!)
❏ A Bus That Could Be the Tour Bus of a Famous Band
Who might it be? _____

❏ UFAs: Unidentified Furry Animals.

Add items to the list!

❏ _____
❏ _____
❏ _____
❏ _____
❏ _____
❏ _____

Billboards

Record the interesting billboards you pass. Or, create your own. What have you got to advertise?

OCTOBER is Squirrel Appreciation MONTH

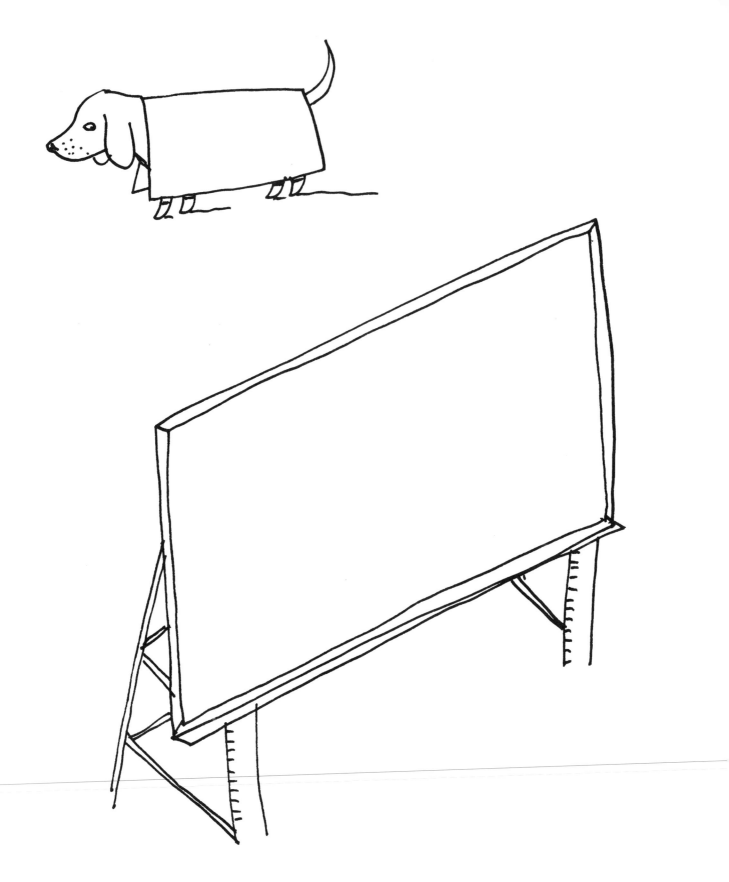

Pick the Worst

Which is worse—finding out there's no milk once you've started eating chocolate-chip cookies or finding out there are no cookies? All of the things below are bad—you decide which is worse. Quiz your travel partners about their choices, too. This quiz can turn major downers into great fun.

1. Which is worse?
❏ Flat soda?   ❏ Hot soda?

2. Which is worse?
❏ Rain on your beach vacation?
❏ No rain and getting a terrible sunburn that forces you to stay indoors?

3. Which is worse?
❏ Bears outside your tent?   ❏ A snake inside it?

4. Which is worse?
❏ Running out of time?   ❏ Running out of money?

5. Which is worse?
❏ Not being in class with your best friend?
❏ Being in class together, but getting in trouble all the time for talking too much?

6. Which is worse?
❏ No heat in the winter?   ❏ No air conditioning in the summer?

7. Which is worse?
❏ Craving something sweet and all you've got is salty?
❏ Biting into something and finding out it's not what you thought it was?

8. Which is worse?
❏ Not getting what you want for your birthday?
❏ Getting what you want and breaking it the first day?

9. Which is worse?
❏ Being submerged in a tub of cockroaches?
❏ Bobbing for rat tails with your teeth?

10. Which is worse?
❏ Not getting tickets to a sports game you really want to see?
❏ Going to the game and watching your team get trounced?

11. Which is worse?
❏ Zombies chasing you?   ❏ A werewolf chasing you?

12. Which is worse?
☐ Hearing a great song on the radio and not knowing who sings it?
☐ Catching the last notes of your favorite song just as it ends?

13. Which is worse?
☐ Not making the school play?   ☐ Getting a good part and flubbing it?

14. Which is worse?
☐ Having to put down a great book just as you're about to get to the end?
☐ Getting to the end and it turns out to be totally disappointing?

15. Which is worse?
☐ Aliens shrink you to the size of a bug?   ☐ Aliens expand you to the size of a giant?

16. Which is worse?
☐ Being called on when you didn't do your homework?
☐ Being called on when you did it but getting the answer wrong?

17. Which is worse?
☐ Mystery meat day at the school cafeteria?   ☐ Asparagus night at home?

18. Which is worse?
☐ Eating fried bugs?   ☐ Eating sautéed snails?

19. Which is worse?
☐ Long car trips with your sibling?   ☐ Long car trips without your sibling?

20. Which is worse?
☐ A spider in your bed?   ☐ A bat on your ceiling?

21. Which is worse?
☐ Smelly feet?   ☐ Bad breath?

22. Which is worse?
☐ Stubbing your toe?   ☐ Biting your tongue?

23. Which is worse?
☐ Snow on a day when there's no school to cancel?
☐ Snow on a school day, but not enough to cancel school?

24. Which is worse?
☐ Getting poison ivy?   ☐ Finding a tick on your body?

25. Which is worse?
☐ Waking up and realizing you've gotten 10 years older overnight?
☐ Waking up and realizing you've gotten younger overnight?

Traffic Jam

Create some congestion by drawing lots of cars, trucks, motorcycles, unicycles...whatever!

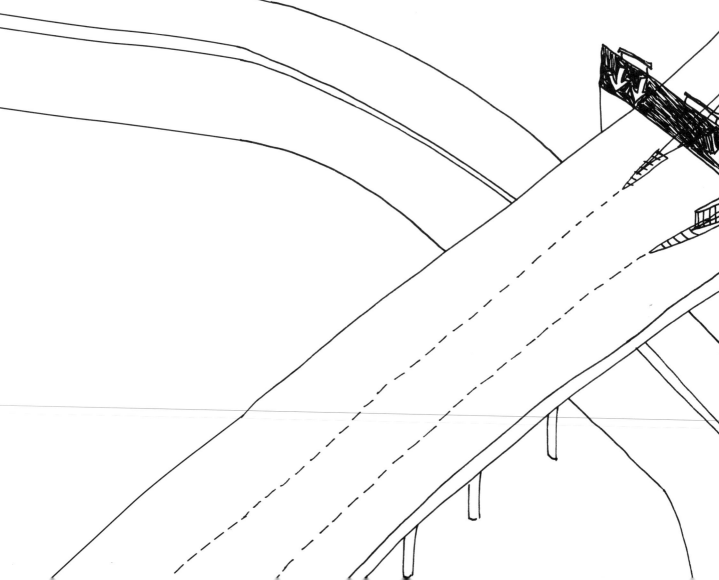

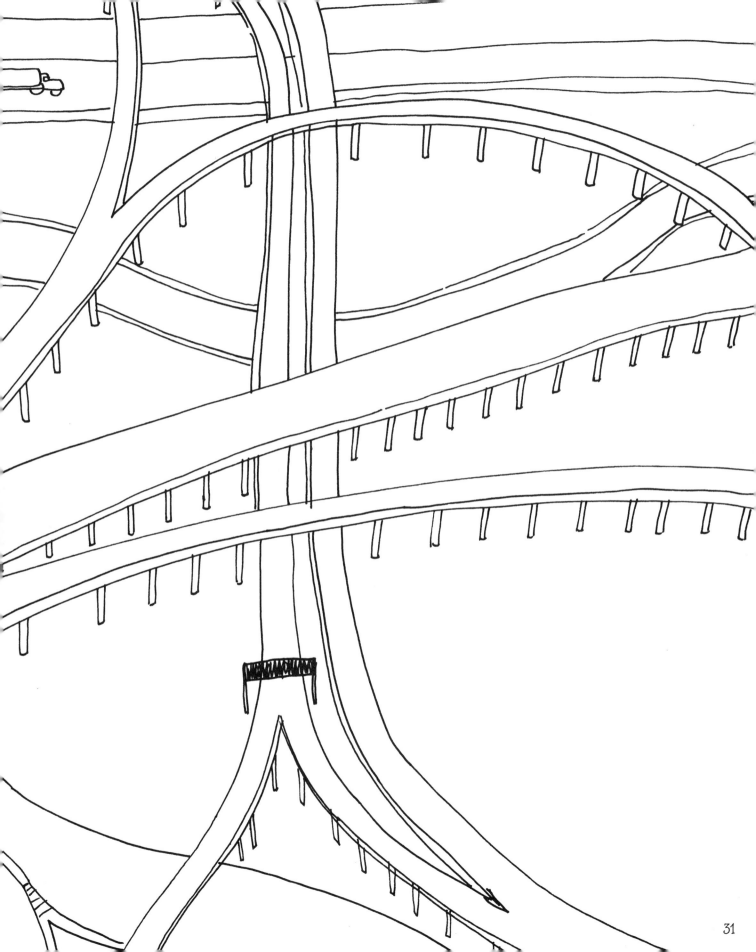

Night Riding

No daylight? No problem. Here are some fun things you can do in the dark.

Padiddle

Padiddle is a game played at night in a car. There's the basic game and lots of variations.

Basic Rules

Players look for cars traveling with only one headlight. Upon finding one, they yell out "Padiddle!" and thump the car ceiling. The single headlight must be seen by at least one other person for it to count, and cars traveling with both headlights turned off don't count.

Points

- A padiddle earns a player a point.
- A motorcycle mistakenly identified as a padiddle subtracts a point.
- If the car in which the game takes place is a padiddle, it can be counted as a padiddle once per game.
- A padiddle on a large truck (more than two axles) earns two points.
- A padiddle on a Hummer earns three points.
- You can also earn a point for a padunkle. A padunkle is a car traveling with one taillight.
- Cars with light-up signs on top (taxis or take-out restaurant cars) are not padiddles, but they can still earn you two points. When you see one you shout, "Take-out car!" or "Taxi!" and claim your points.
- Whoever has the most points when you reach your destination (or stop for the night) wins.

Padiddles of the Past

Paddidle has actually been around since the time before cars. It's said that the game started in the days when carriages lit by candle lanterns were the primary means of transportation. There were many superstitions about candles that had blown out or burned down. To see one was considered bad luck, so a person would kiss the person next to him for good luck. (Kissing is still part of the way some people play the game today.)

Paddidle is played all over North America, and has different names in different regions. In the South, it's often called Perdiddle; in the West, it's sometimes called Padoodle or Perdido. Other ways to play the game have sprung up, too. Some variations say that you should punch your neighbor in the shoulder when you say padiddle, instead of hitting the roof of the car. But you didn't hear that from us.

North Star Navigator

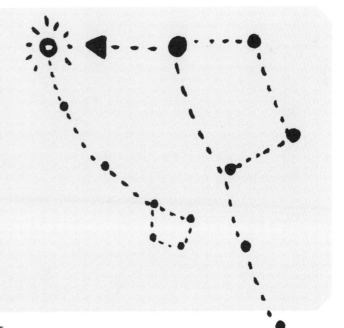

In the old days, travelers used the stars to help them navigate at night. The "North Star" or Polaris, is one of the brightest stars in the night sky, and it's said to be in a fixed position that always indicates "true north." If you can figure out where Polaris is, you can figure out the other directions as well.

Try to find the North Star if your family stops for a break at night. First you'll need to find the Big Dipper. Locate the "pointer" stars on the end of the dipper's bowl. They will point you toward the North Star, which is the last star in the Little Dipper's handle.

Guggenheim

SPORTS

Ah, Guggenheim. It's the name of a great museum in New York City and a fun word game that can be played anytime, anywhere, with no more than two players required. You'll be surprised by how quickly you'll get hooked on it!

How to Play

This game can be played with any number of participants.

- *Use the grids on the opposite page to play. Make copies of the grid on the blank pages at the back of this book for future games. As you can see, the column on the far left is just wide enough for one capital letter. The row at the top is only tall and wide enough for one word. The other columns are big enough that you can write a list of words inside.*

- The game starts with each player choosing a five-letter word. Write the word vertically in the column on the left, one letter per box.

- Next, players choose categories to go in the row across the top. The categories can be anything the players want, but all players should try to agree on them.

- Here are some suggestions: Movies, Books, Famous People, Sports, Songs, Actors/Actresses, Animals, Authors, Food, Countries.

- Players decide on a time limit, usually between 15 and 30 minutes. When time starts, all players try to list as many items under each letter of each category as possible.

- Let's say the five-letter word in the first column was "shirt," and the first category was "movies." You could write "Shrek" in the first box, "Homeward Bound" in the second box, "Indiana Jones" in the third box, "Rugrats" in the fourth box, and "The Incredibles" in the fifth box. Not as easy as it looks, huh? That's why you'll need a good word for the first column—something with lots of commonly used letters.

- You and your fellow players will have to agree on some rules. For example, if the category is authors or famous people, will the person's first or last name qualify? Will you count the word "the" or pronouns in front of a title? Just make sure you agree before you start to play.

- You'll get points for each unique word you come up with. So if two players both come up with "Shrek," neither will get points for it. Decide on the number of points (usually 10) for each unique word.

BOOKS   COUNTRIES   FOOD   ANIMALS

Here's an example. Can you finish it?

	Authors	Countries	Elements	Songs	Relatives
S	Shakespeare Shelley	Spain			
T	Tolkien	Turkey			
R	Rowling	Romania			
A	Asimov Anderson	Australia Austria Afghanistan			
P	Pohl	Poland			

The Hidden You

Can your answers to some simple questions reveal the true, inner you? Some psychologists think so. Try taking these quizzes on the next four pages and answering honestly. Then turn to page 246 to find out what your answers say about you. Don't worry if the answers aren't what you thought they would be. These quizzes are more fun than serious, but you might be surprised at some things they do get right! After you've learned about yourself, it's fun to give the quiz to someone else—just make sure you don't reveal any of the answers beforehand! You can compare notes!

A Walk in the Woods

For this quiz, you'll need to imagine the scenes and write down or say aloud the FIRST thing you visualize. It's important that your answer be spontaneous—in other words, don't think about it too much.

1. You are walking and you come to a forest. Describe the forest—big, small, what kind of trees, etc.

   _____

   _____

2. There is a path going into the forest. Describe the path.

   _____

   _____

3. Along the path, you find a key. What do you do with it? Describe what it looks like.

   _____

   _____

4. Next, you come to an obstacle in the path. What is it? How do you get past it?

   _____

   _____

5. You see a house. Describe what it looks like.

   _____

   _____

6. In the house, you find a room that's all white with no windows. How do you feel when you're inside the room?

   _____

   _____

Ask friends or family to give it a try! They can write their answers here.

 1. You are walking and you come to a forest. Describe the forest—big, small, what kind of trees, etc.

_____

_____

2. There is a path going into the forest. Describe the path.

_____

3. Along the path, you find a key. What do you do with it? Describe what it looks like.

_____

_____

4. Next, you come to an obstacle in the path. What is it? How do you get past it?

_____

_____

5. You see a house. Describe what it looks like.

_____

_____

6. In the house, you find a room that's all white with no windows. How do you feel when you're inside the room?

_____

_____

1. You are walking and you come to a forest. Describe the forest—big, small, what kind of trees, etc.

_____

2. There is a path going into the forest. Describe the path.

_____

3. Along the path, you find a key. What do you do with it? Describe what it looks like.

_____

_____

4. Next, you come to an obstacle in the path. What is it? How do you get past it?

_____

5. You see a house. Describe what it looks like.

_____

6. In the house, you find a room that's all white with no windows. How do you feel when you're inside the room?

_____

_____

A Walk in the Desert

 You are in a desert. These five animals are with you: a lion, a cow, a horse, a sheep, and a monkey. To cross the desert successfully, you are going to have to get rid of one of your animals. Answers are on page 246.

1. Which one do you leave behind first? To decide, you can use whatever logic you want.

   _____

2. You have four animals left. The desert is burning hot. You grow more tired. You have to leave behind another animal. Which do you choose next?

   _____

3. You have three animals left. Walk, walk, walk. Hot, hot, hot. There is no oasis in sight. You have no choice but to leave behind another animal. Which is the next to go?

   _____

4. You have two animals left. Finally, you see the edge of the desert on the horizon. But you can only keep one animal. Which do you keep? _____
   Which one goes? _____

Now ask friends or family to give it a try!

You are in a desert. These five animals are with you: a lion, a cow, a horse, a sheep, and a monkey. To cross the desert successfully, you are going to have to get rid of one of your animals.

1. Which one do you leave behind first? To decide, you can use whatever logic you want.

   _____

2. You have four animals left. The desert is burning hot. You grow more tired.
   You have to leave behind another animal. Which do you choose next?

   _____

3. You have three animals left. Walk, walk, walk. Hot, hot, hot. There is no oasis in sight.
   You have no choice but to leave behind another animal. Which is the next to go?

   _____

4. You have two animals left. Finally, you see the edge of the desert on the horizon. But you can only keep one animal. Which do you keep? _____
   Which one goes? _____

You are in a desert. These five animals are with you: a lion, a cow, a horse, a sheep, and a monkey. To cross the desert successfully, you are going to have to get rid of one of your animals.

1. Which one do you leave behind first? To decide, you can use whatever logic you want.

   _____

2. You have four animals left. The desert is burning hot. You grow more tired.
   You have to leave behind another animal. Which do you choose next?

   _____

3. You have three animals left. Walk, walk, walk. Hot, hot, hot. There is no oasis in sight.
   You have no choice but to leave behind another animal. Which is the next to go?

   _____

4. You have two animals left. Finally, you see the edge of the desert on the horizon. But you can only keep one animal. Which do you keep? _____
   Which one goes? _____

Rebus Puzzles

When you try a rebus puzzle, you need to:

```
_____
read
_____
```

Got that? "Read between the lines." A rebus puzzle is a kind of word puzzle that combines pictures and words to represent a word or expression. See if you can decipher these tricky turns of phrase. *Use the blank boxes to create your own.* Answers on page 246.

stefrankin

1. _____

ICE^3

2. _____

momanon

3. _____

M1LLION

4. _____

9S2A5F4E1T8Y6

5. _____

go it it it it

6. _____

Nooutwhere

7. _____

calm storm

8. _____

me right

9. _____

lang4uage

10. _____

head
heels

11. _____

travel
cccccccc

12. _____

O
O

13. _____

BROTHER

14. _____

SKATING
ICE

15. _____

man
board

16. _____

D A N C E
A   C
N   N
C   A
E C N A D

17. _____

s h o e
    o w r
s h o
    h w e r

18. _____

issue issue issue
issue issue issue
issue issue issue
issue

19. _____

tario
Lake

20. _____

sgeg

21. _____

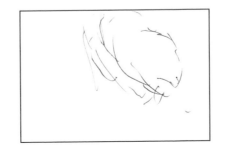

22. _____

23. _____

24. _____

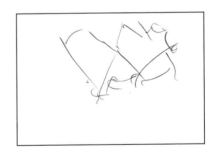

25. _____

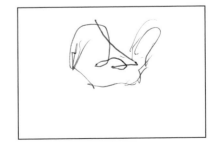

26. _____

Travel Cootie Catcher

Haven't you always wanted to know how to make a cootie catcher? Now is your chance! Follow these easy instructions and you'll have instant entertainment at your fingertips. All you need is a piece of paper. Use a blank page from the back of the book if you want.

1. To turn a rectangular piece of paper into a square, fold the bottom left corner of the paper up to the right side of the page. Cut or tear off the flap above the triangle. Unfold the paper so you have a square with a diagonal crease across the middle.

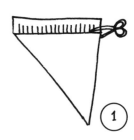

2. Fold the bottom right corner of the square to the top left corner diagonally.

3. Unfold the paper. Now your creases will look like an X.

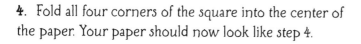

4. Fold all four corners of the square into the center of the paper. Your paper should now look like step 4.

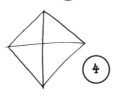

5. Flip the square. The folded sides should be facedown. Repeat step 4 for this side of the paper. Now your paper will have folds on both sides.

6. The creases and folds you made should create eight triangles on one side. Number them 1 through 8.

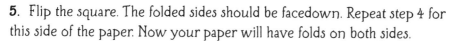

7. Fold the square in half. Then unfold it.

8. Fold the paper in half in the other direction and open it again. The numbers you've written should be facing you.

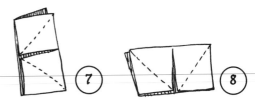
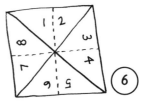

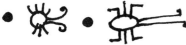

9. Now the fun part! Open each flap and write a fortune on it. *Use the ones below or make up your own.* Close all the flaps when you're finished.

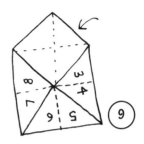

Travel Fortunes

- You will get the window seat next time.
- You will meet someone special on this trip.
- There will be an interesting surprise under your pillow tonight.
- Don't drink the water!
- There is a delicious treat in your future.
- Don't order the cheeseburger.
- Don't forget to write home.
- Today is your lucky day.
- Tomorrow will be your lucky day.
- He who does not whine will be first in line.
- You should have brought a rain jacket.

10. Flip the paper. On each square, draw a different colored dot.

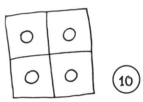

11. Flip the paper again. (The numbers should be face up.) Fold the square in half and slide your fingers under the four flaps. The cootie catcher should expand as you bring your thumb and index finger together. The numbered triangles will disappear inside.

How to Use It

Each player chooses a color. Open and close the cootie catcher, one time for every letter of the color, lengthwise, and then widthwise. Have a player select one of the numbers that appears in the center. Open and close the cootie catcher that number of times. When you stop, open it up to reveal the numbers. Ask the player to pick one of the four flaps. Read the player's fortune.

Palm Reading

Long journey, hours to go, nothing to do but look at your hands? That might be a lot more interesting than you think. Since ancient times and in cultures around the world, people have believed that the arrangement of the lines on your hand holds clues to your destiny. What does your future hold? Take a stab at reading your own palm to find out. Reading your palm is a little tougher than reading a book, but it won't make you car sick.

A Quick Lesson in Palm Reading

If you're left-handed, read your left hand. If you're right-handed, read your right hand. Keep this in mind if you're reading someone else's hand.

Everyone has the same kinds of lines on their hands, but each person's lines are unique. Your lines might be longer, shorter, stronger, or fainter than the ones shown on the map. In other words, if you can't find your life line, don't worry, it doesn't mean you're dead! It might just look different from the one you see here.

Heart Line

Locate your heart line. This is the line that governs your emotions. If it is high and far away from the head line, it means you are a very passionate person—you don't do things half way. If you like or love something or someone, you do it with all your heart.

If your line is closer to the head line, it means you're very levelheaded and balanced.

If your heart line is quite curvy it means you're outgoing. If it's straighter, it means you keep your feelings more to yourself.

Head Line

Locate your head line. If it's a strong line, it means you're focused on getting what you want. If the line is faint, it means you're indecisive.

Life Line

Contrary to what you might have heard, the life line doesn't tell how long you'll live, but rather gives clues about how you'll live your life. If it's rather straight and connects to your head

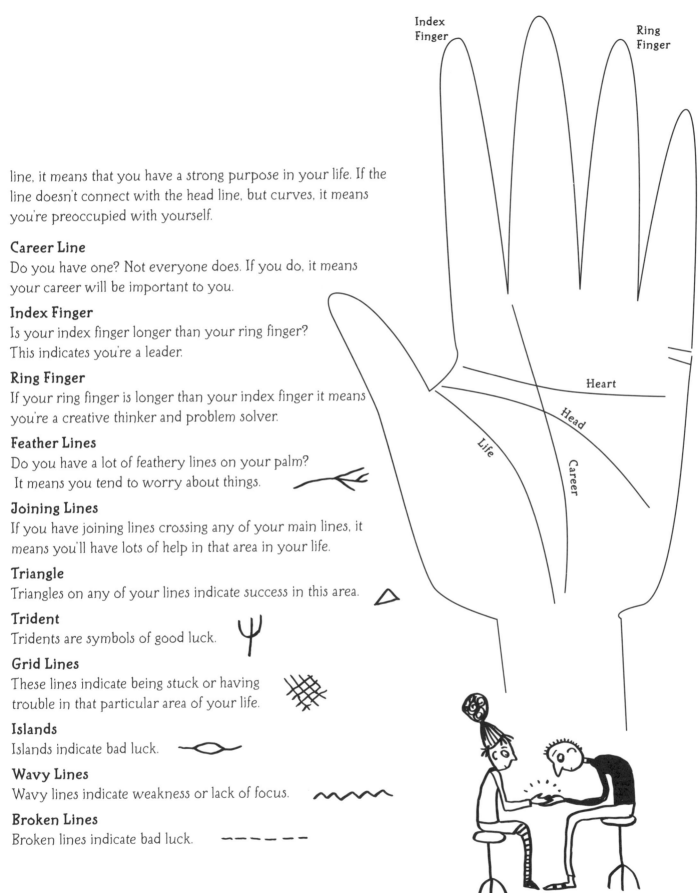

line, it means that you have a strong purpose in your life. If the line doesn't connect with the head line, but curves, it means you're preoccupied with yourself.

Career Line
Do you have one? Not everyone does. If you do, it means your career will be important to you.

Index Finger
Is your index finger longer than your ring finger? This indicates you're a leader.

Ring Finger
If your ring finger is longer than your index finger it means you're a creative thinker and problem solver.

Feather Lines
Do you have a lot of feathery lines on your palm? It means you tend to worry about things.

Joining Lines
If you have joining lines crossing any of your main lines, it means you'll have lots of help in that area in your life.

Triangle
Triangles on any of your lines indicate success in this area.

Trident
Tridents are symbols of good luck.

Grid Lines
These lines indicate being stuck or having trouble in that particular area of your life.

Islands
Islands indicate bad luck.

Wavy Lines
Wavy lines indicate weakness or lack of focus.

Broken Lines
Broken lines indicate bad luck.

45

Draw These Animals

Follow these steps and you'll end up with perfect biological specimens.
Well, actually, you'll end up with some silly, scribbly animals.

Desert Explorer's Journal

You've been spending time exploring in the desert. Here is a record of your findings. Now draw in pictures of your discoveries.

The Hammerhead Snake

A snake with a head resembling a hammerhead shark, with one eye on the end of each "hammer." Has strange, triangular markings down its back and a "Y" shaped tail.

The Weeping Cactus

A tall cactus with "weeping arms" that bend over toward the ground, similar to a weeping willow tree. Can be found under rocky cliffs.

The Prairie Cat
Lives in holes, just like prairie dogs, but has
whiskers and a tail, and likes to cuddle.

The Camule
Camel-like animal with long mule-like ears and tail.

What else did you find?

Cartoon Captions

We drew 'em...you make 'em funny!

Hangman

Use the gallows on these pages to play this oldie but goodie!

Don't know how to play? No problem!

- One player secretly thinks of a word and draws blanks under one of the gallows to represent its letters.

- The other player begins guessing the letters, one at a time. If the letter is correct, the first player writes it wherever it appears in the blanks. If the guess is wrong, the first player starts drawing a person hanging from the noose, one body part at a time: head, body, left arm, right arm, left leg, right leg. (You can agree to add more details such as hands and feet to keep the game going longer.)

- A player can guess the word instead of a letter. If he gets it right, he wins. If not, and a complete figure is drawn on the gallows—the hangman wins.

What's the Point?

Use only dots to create your drawing. No lines.
Your travel mates will exclaim, "Dot's amazing!"

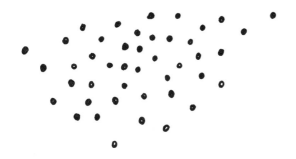

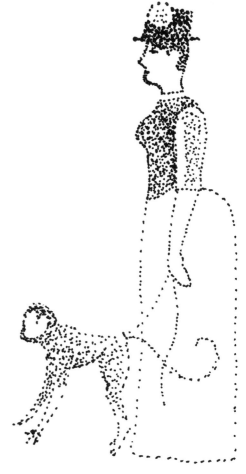

Gridlock

Just as crossroads intersect, you'll create a puzzle with words that cross each other. Keep playing until the intersections are jammed.

- Decide on a category of words that will be allowed in the grid. It could be anything from favorite foods to cars to song titles, or simply animal, vegetable, or mineral.
- The first player writes down her word, making sure one letter of it is inside one of the center squares.
- Player two now thinks of a second word with at least one letter in common with the first word and adds it to the grid so it "crosses" with the first word.
- A player gets a point for each letter of his word, except for the letter "crossing" another word. So, long words are better.
- Continue crossing words in the category until you're gridlocked and no more can fit in the grid. Whoever has the most points wins.
- Use the blank pages in the back of this book to make smaller or bigger grids.

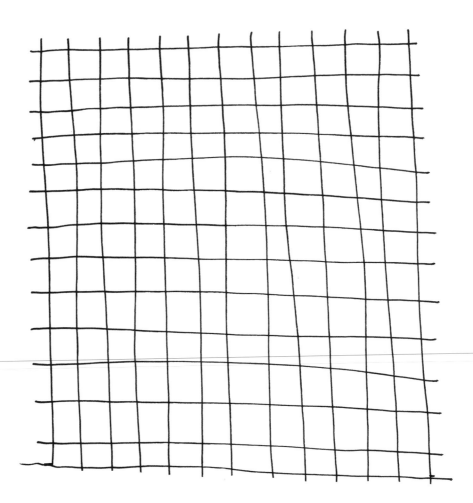

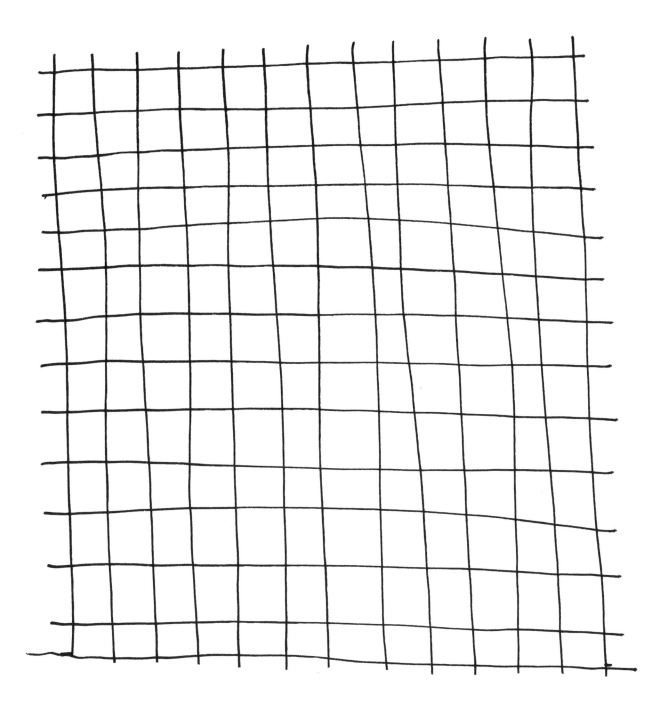

Are-ay Ou-yay Aving-hay Un-fay Et-yay?

Have you always wanted to learn another language? Why not start now? You can be practically fluent in Pig Latin by the time you get to your destination. Pig Latin is a secret language, often used when the speaker doesn't want certain listeners to understand what's being said (kind of like when your parents used to spell out words before you knew how to read). It may seem hard at first, but once you've practiced a bit, ou-yay ill-way e-bay able-ay oo-tay ead-ray is-thay.

Here are the basic rules of Pig Latin

If a word begins with consonants, move the consonants to the end of the word. Then add "ay" after the consonant.

For example:

School = ool-schay

Drive = ive-dray

Happy = appy-hay

Sleep = eep-slay

Want = Ant-way

If a word begins with a vowel sound or a silent consonant, there are two ways to do it. You can just add the "ay" to the end.

For example:

I = I-ay

Ask = Ask-ay

Or, instead of just adding "ay," you can add another consonant that sounds good (usually y, w, or h).

Add = Add-hay

Another = Another-yay

If you wanted to say "Stop kicking me or I will tell Mom and Dad" in Pig Latin, you would say:

"Op-stay icking-kay e-may or-hay I-yay ill-way ell-tay Om-may and-way Ad-day."

It may sound tough, but the more you do it in your head, the easier it will become.

Other Secret Languages

S Language

The secret of the S language is given away right there in the title, but it's easier to learn than Pig Latin!

Here's how it works:

Choose a word to be translated: "Hello," for example.

Break it into syllables. This one has two; "he" and "lo."

Add the "s" sound at the end of each syllable and repeat whichever vowel sound ends the syllable: "heseloso."

Ubbi Dubbi

Ubbi Dubbi (also called Double Dutch or Pig Greek) may take you a little while to master, but sounds wonderful when spoken well!

To speak Ubbi Dubbi, you add an "ub" before the vowels of each syllable in a word.

For example, speak = spubeak.

So a question might be:

"Dubo yubou spubeak Ubbi Dubbi?"

Elephant

Elephant is similar to Ubbi Dubbi, except you add the "eleph" before every vowel.

So, "Let's talk" would be, "Lelephet's telephalk."

This language won't get you far with pachyderms, but it does make a big mouthful. Try saying this fast:

"ElephI welephish elephI knelephew selephomelephethelephing scelephandelephalelephoelephus."

This Land Is Your Land

Imaginary countries are fun to visit while on the way to your real destination. Here's a map of an imaginary land, ready for you to explore. All that's known about it is what you see here: the lines of its borders and coastline; the locations of a few mountains and rivers. The rest is left for you to fill in. You can give the country cities, lakes, rivers, more mountains, volcanoes—whatever you like. Where is the capital and what is it called? Where are the roads and highways? What are the names of the bordering countries?

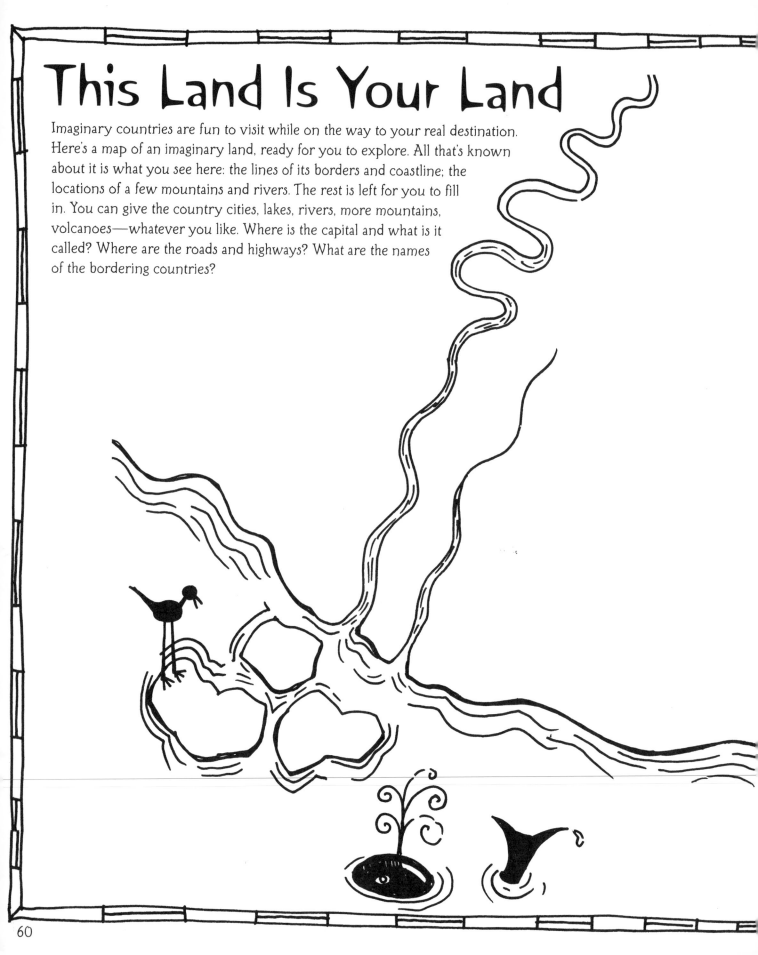

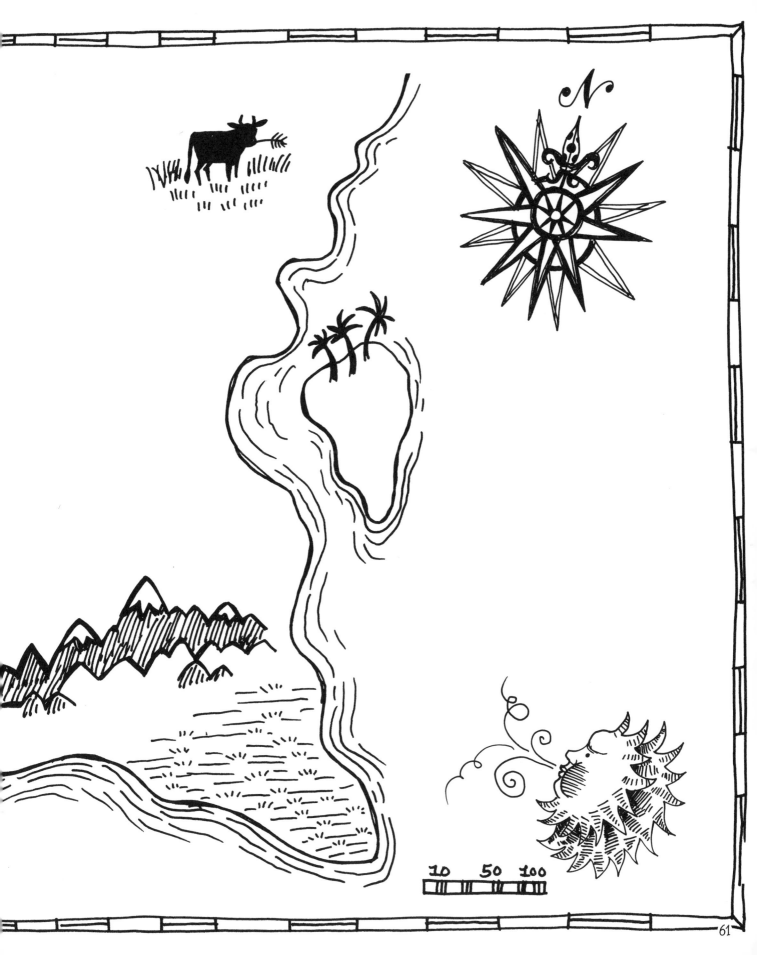

Notes from the Creator

On the last two pages you created a new world. Now you have to fill in the details. Failure to do so would be irresponsible. How would your inhabitants live without this important information?

Your country's name _____

Name of its inhabitants _____

Language spoken _____

How you say "Hello" in the language _____

How you say "Thank you" _____

How you say "How are you?" _____

"What's your name?" _____

"Where can I find cheese?" _____

Translate some of your favorite phrases _____

_____

_____

_____

_____

_____

_____

Currency (What's the name of the money the country uses?) _____

Draw pictures of the currency here:

Draw some inhabitants:

3414 Apt 206

Hillcrest Hgts

Maryland

Washington D.C.

United States of America

go to mall and play on playground

Nice people, like to go out and party

Allyson my roommate likes to go to work

And so does my mom. Allison Pittman or A.P.

is from NYC. My mom is from Ethiopia

by way of San leandro, CA.

Create a flag for your country.

Tell a little bit about your country here: How do the people of your country spend their time? What are they like—friendly, warlike, nomadic, settled, fond of cheese? Are there any legends about how your country came to be? Any famous rulers or heroes and heroines in the past?

_____

_____

_____

_____

_____

_____

_____

_____

_____

_____

_____

_____

_____

_____

_____

Don't Stop

Put your pencil tip on the page and don't lift it until you have completed a drawing.
Do it over and over again.

Sonic Scavenger Hunt

Just how good of a listener are you? Play this game to find out. This scavenger hunt has a twist—you have to use your ears instead of your eyes. It's best played on long car trips with the radio on. You'll get three points for each sound you collect, as well as extra points if you can answer additional questions. Keep track of your own sonic discoveries, or share the list with your travel partners for more of a challenge—whoever hears an entry first gets an extra point.

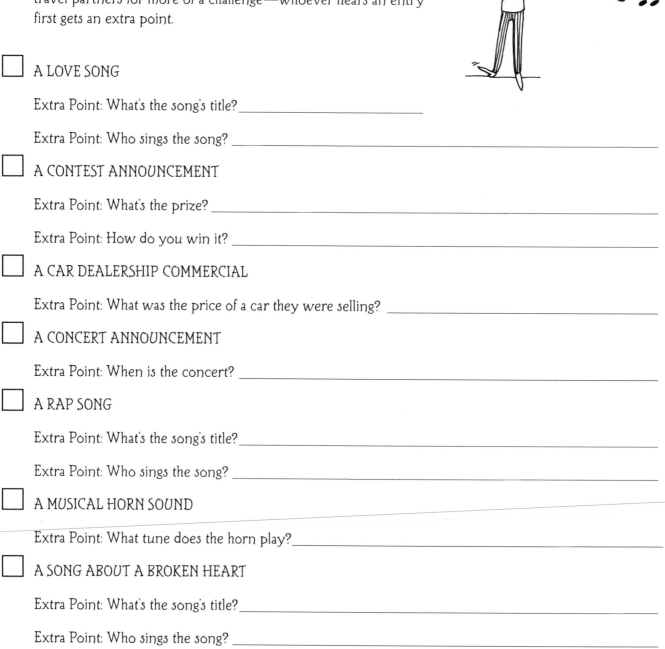

☐ A LOVE SONG

Extra Point: What's the song's title? _____

Extra Point: Who sings the song? _____

☐ A CONTEST ANNOUNCEMENT

Extra Point: What's the prize? _____

Extra Point: How do you win it? _____

☐ A CAR DEALERSHIP COMMERCIAL

Extra Point: What was the price of a car they were selling? _____

☐ A CONCERT ANNOUNCEMENT

Extra Point: When is the concert? _____

☐ A RAP SONG

Extra Point: What's the song's title? _____

Extra Point: Who sings the song? _____

☐ A MUSICAL HORN SOUND

Extra Point: What tune does the horn play? _____

☐ A SONG ABOUT A BROKEN HEART

Extra Point: What's the song's title? _____

Extra Point: Who sings the song? _____

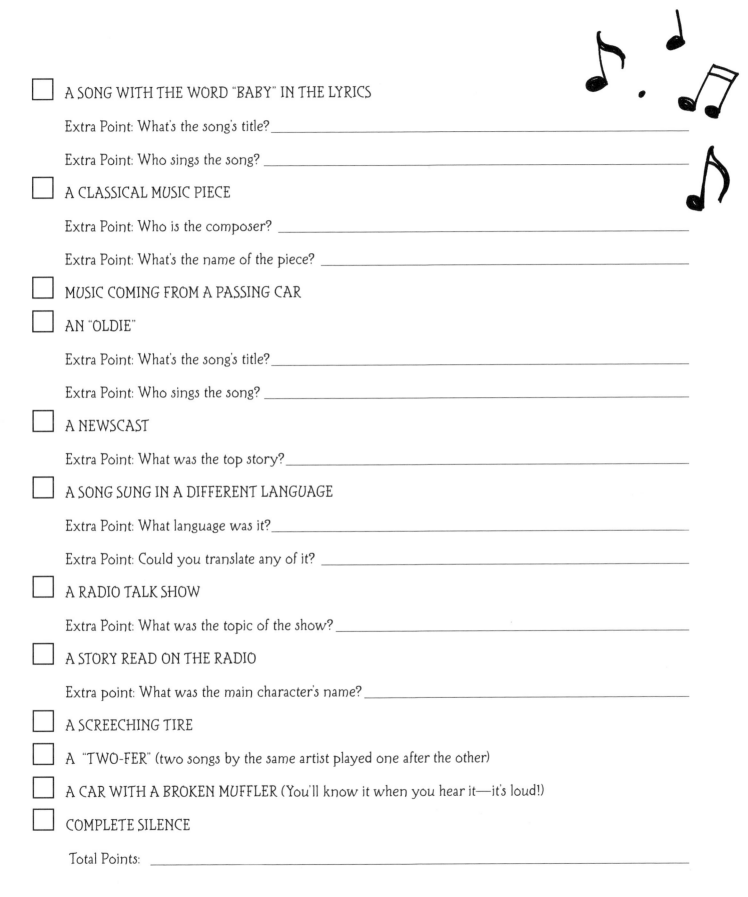

☐ A SONG WITH THE WORD "BABY" IN THE LYRICS

Extra Point: What's the song's title? _____

Extra Point: Who sings the song? _____

☐ A CLASSICAL MUSIC PIECE

Extra Point: Who is the composer? _____

Extra Point: What's the name of the piece? _____

☐ MUSIC COMING FROM A PASSING CAR

☐ AN "OLDIE"

Extra Point: What's the song's title? _____

Extra Point: Who sings the song? _____

☐ A NEWSCAST

Extra Point: What was the top story? _____

☐ A SONG SUNG IN A DIFFERENT LANGUAGE

Extra Point: What language was it? _____

Extra Point: Could you translate any of it? _____

☐ A RADIO TALK SHOW

Extra Point: What was the topic of the show? _____

☐ A STORY READ ON THE RADIO

Extra point: What was the main character's name? _____

☐ A SCREECHING TIRE

☐ A "TWO-FER" (two songs by the same artist played one after the other)

☐ A CAR WITH A BROKEN MUFFLER (You'll know it when you hear it—it's loud!)

☐ COMPLETE SILENCE

Total Points: _____

Bumper Match

Bumper stickers can be serious business, but the best kinds are those that give you just a little chuckle when you read them. Here's a collection of some of the silliest ones out there. Match the first part of the phrase with its punch line by drawing a line between the two. Some will make you laugh out loud and others might leave you scratching your head until you get to your destination. Answers on page 246.

Earth First.	Where Would You Put It?
You Can't Have Everything.	If Anything Falls Off
The More People I Meet,	Is a Broom
This Would Be Really Funny	What You Can Avoid Doing Altogether
A Day Without Sunshine	Are Hard to Find
What If the Hokey Pokey	But I'm Ahead of You
Honk	And Other Creatures Only I Can See
If at First You Don't Succeed,	Buy One in Every Color
Caution! I Brake for Elves, Fairies, Unicorns,	I'm Lost Too
My Other Car	IS What It's All About?
Please Hit Me	Is Like Night
Don't Follow Me	No Apparent Reason
Minds Are Like Parachutes—	The More I Like My Dog
Never Put Off Till Tomorrow	If It Weren't Happening to Me
My Other Car	Then Skydiving Is Not for You
If the Shoe Fits,	They Work Best When Open
I May Be Slow	We'll Log the Other Planets Later
I Brake for	Is a Spaceship
Good Planets	So I Can Get a New Car

Make Your Own

Can you come up with some witty one-liners on your own?

Fast Food

Don't eat it—draw it! Ask someone to time you. You have two minutes to draw pictures of as many types of food as you can think of on these pages.

Hair Today

These heads all have something in common. They need hair. And you're just the person for the job.

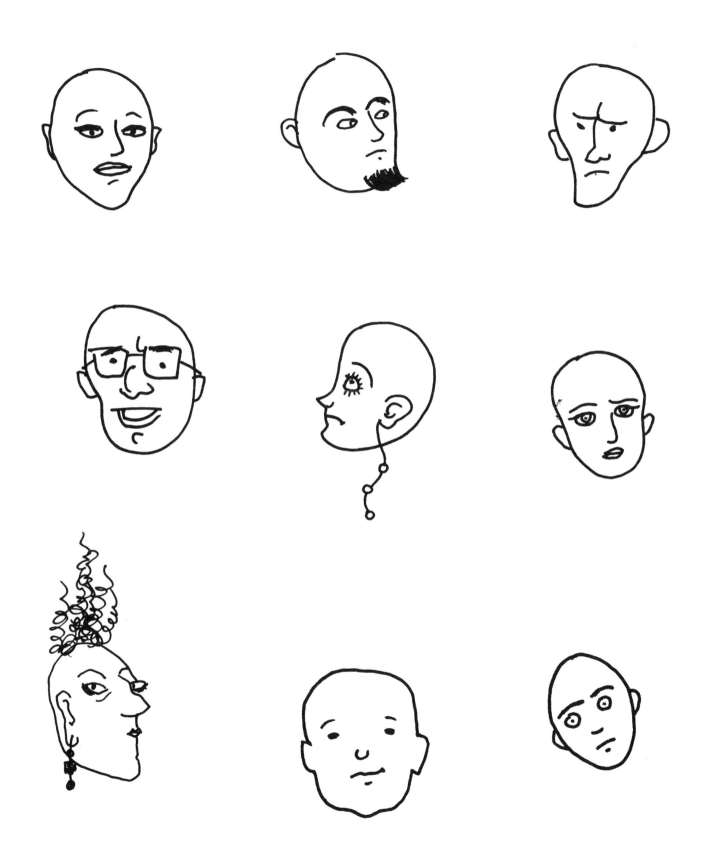

One to Ten

Rank these things from 1 to 10, 1 being your favorite, 10 being at the bottom of the pile.

Colors

Black

Blue

Pink

Red

Yellow

Orange

Purple

Brown

White

Green

Food

Pizza

Oranges

Popcorn

Hamburgers

Peanut butter and jelly

Grilled cheese

Ice cream

Apples

Grapes

Macaroni and cheese

Flavors

Spicy

Salty

Sweet

Sour

Chewy

Crunchy

Smooth

Fruity

Gooey

Doughy

Animals

Dog

Bear

Cat

Panda

Lion

Zebra

Giraffe

Seal

Elephant

Bunny

Games

Chess

Go Fish

Backgammon

Tag

Poker

Video games

Truth or Dare

Go

Charades

Checkers

Sports

Tennis
Swimming
Ice skating
Soccer
Hockey
Baseball
Football
Basketball
Snowboarding
Skateboarding

Places

The beach
The woods
The mountains
The playing field/court
The library
My room
My backyard
School
An airplane
On stage

School Subjects

English
Science
Math
Gym
Recess
Art
Social Studies
Music
History
Computers

Things

My games
My bed
My pet
My favorite outfit
My collection
My electronic stuff
My diary
My report cards
My books
My craft supplies

Me

My sense of humor
My brain
My special talent
My personality
My attitude
My heritage
My beliefs
My voice
My hopes and dreams
My toes

Art Car!

Have you ever almost climbed into the wrong car in the school pick-up line? One beige minivan looks pretty much like the next, doesn't it? But if you had an art car, there'd be no mistaking which super-cool, completely unique vehicle was yours. An art car is an ordinary car transformed into a work of art with paint, beads, recycled materials, junk, toys, fake grass, stickers, silk flower petals—just about anything a creative driver or passenger can dream up. Headlights turn into eyes if you just paint eyelashes on top of them. How about a tail on your trunk?

Turn this ordinary car into an art car!

Now draw your real car here. Then turn it into an art car.

Get Your Art Car Inspiration in Gear

Make your car into an animal, real or imaginary.
Try a pig, dog, cat, shark, dragon, fish, or deer. Add a tail on the end, fins on the doors, antlers on the roof, a snout on the hood. Change the rearview mirror into eyes, or add teeth to the front bumper.

Leave the road behind—make your car into a spaceship! Add flames on the side, probe devices coming out of the tires, and rockets wherever you like.

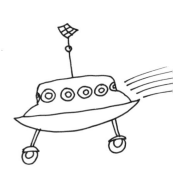

Ahoy, matey! Make your car into a pirate ship!

Green your car! Add petals, flowers, blossoms, or leaves.

Pick a theme: the beach, dinosaurs, mummies, or monsters.
Design and decorate a car according to your theme.

Got the T-Shirt

Been there, done that, got the T-shirt—it's one of those sayings you hear all the time when people talk about their experiences. What would the T-shirt from your trip look like? Use these pages to design one or more. Make up a slogan and a logo that captures the highlight of your trip.

MY
PARENTS
WENT TO
GRACELAND
AND ALL I
GOT WAS THIS
STUPID T-SHIRT

Fact or Fiction?

Can you really get a can of soda for free if you pour saltwater into a drink machine's coin slot? Can the Great Wall of China really be seen from outer space? Take this quiz to find out how good you are at separating fact from fiction. Answers on page 247.

1. Beware of the chocolate bar! If you have a dog, keep him away from your Halloween candy! Dogs can die from eating chocolate.
☐ True   ☐ False

2. Think twice before you use that gas-station bathroom. South American blush spiders, which have a poisonous bite and live in cool, damp places, have been found under toilet seats in public restrooms.
☐ True   ☐ False

3. If you pour saltwater into the coin slot of a soda machine, free soda cans will come out of the machine.
☐ True   ☐ False

4. In Alaska, an eagle swooped down and flew away with someone's dog.
☐ True   ☐ False

5. Bananas imported from Costa Rica contain flesh-eating bacteria.
☐ True   ☐ False

6. Alligators live in the sewers of New York City. They got there when people with pet baby alligators flushed them down the toilet when they grew too big to be cute.
☐ True   ☐ False

7. A Japanese bank received a thank you note from the criminals who robbed it.
☐ True   ☐ False

8. A Pennsylvania flea market patron found an original copy of the Declaration of Independence beneath a picture he purchased for $4.
☐ True   ☐ False

9. Tourists who have taken rocks from Hawaiian beaches return home to find that they are cursed with bad luck.
☐ True   ☐ False

10. Snakes have been found in the ball pits of play areas at some fast-food restaurants.
☐ True   ☐ False

11. A family vacationing in Mexico brought back a rare cactus. A few weeks later, they noticed the cactus was vibrating. The father contacted the Department of Agriculture, who put him in touch with a cactus expert. The expert told the man to get himself and his family out of the house as soon as possible because the cactus was full of huge tarantulas and was about to explode.
❏ True   ❏ False

12. It took 90 minutes for firefighters to free a New York man who got his hand stuck in a commuter train toilet while trying to retrieve his cell phone, which had fallen in the bowl.
❏ True   ❏ False

13. The number of people alive today is greater than the number of people who have ever died.
❏ True   ❏ False

14. Cockroaches can crawl in your ears and get stuck in your earwax.
❏ True   ❏ False

15. A rock climber lost her contact lens as she was hanging from a rope on the edge of a cliff. At the end of her climb, when she returned to the bottom of the canyon, someone spotted an ant walking by carrying the lens.
❏ True   ❏ False

16. A man attached a bunch of weather balloons to a lawn chair and floated up into the flight path of jets leaving the Los Angeles airport. He stayed afloat for 14 hours until rescued by a helicopter.
❏ True   ❏ False

17. The Great Wall of China is the only manmade structure visible from outer space.
❏ True   ❏ False

18. The nursery rhyme "Sing a Song of Sixpence" was a coded message used to recruit pirates.
❏ True   ❏ False

How Insulting!

Finish the insults below any way you want. Take turns writing these with your travel mates, and have fun reading them out loud. Remember, this is about getting a good laugh and not about crushing someone like a bug.

I can't tell what's dripping out of your nose. I hope it isn't

_____.

The Dork Club inducted you as a high-ranking member because

_____

_____.

Your _____ smells

like a jar of _____ that

spent the day in the sun.

Today your _____

reminds me of something

I stepped in

( ) at the zoo.

( ) behind the circus.

( ) in a dark alley.

Was that you I saw on "Lifestyles

of the _____ and

_____" last night?

They wouldn't let you into

the store because the sign said:

"No _____

No _____

No Service."

Your _____ is repulsive.

However, your _____ is quite

attractive—if you're a _____.

_____ has a very

strong _____ smell with

a delicate whiff of _____.

You're not entirely _____.

You do have some redeeming qualities.

For instance, _____.

You snore so loudly that the people of

_____, miles away,

are convinced giant _____

live in the sky.

You tried to enter a _____

contest, but the judges said,

"No _____."

_____'s face can now be seen on
( ) the one-tenth cent piece.
( ) a counterfeit bill.
( ) federal garbage trucks.
( ) _____.

Too bad you weren't born in a

barn. That would explain why you

_____ like a _____.

Scientists used a robotic arm to clean

your _____. Even the

robot said, "_____!"

You're not from this planet. Your

_____ and _____

could never have formed in the

Earth's atmosphere.

Have I mentioned your_____?
It's
( ) malodorous.
( ) preposterous.
( ) disastrous.

Even _____ run away

from you, because they fear

_____.

Cityscape

All roads lead to somewhere. Draw the city that's at the end of the roads.

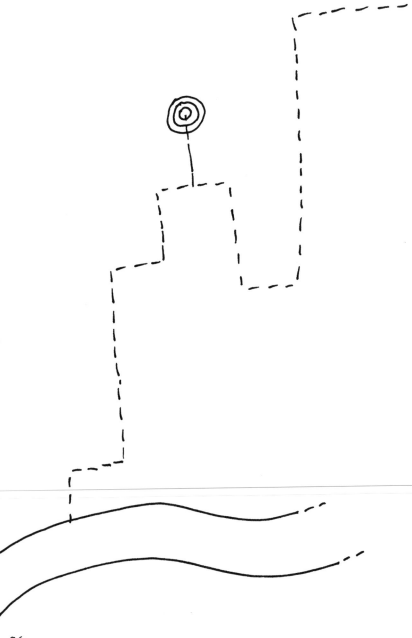

Traveling under an Assumed Identity

Lots of celebrities leave their real names behind when they travel. Although you might not get recognized quite as much as they do, it's fun to have an alter ego when you travel. Something daring, like a pirate name? Out of this world, like a video-game character name? Try one on and see how you like it.

Pirate Name

Want to inspire fear in your siblings while traveling? Discover your pirate name and let your inner pirate swashbuckle his way through the trip.

Your Title

Find your title, based on your birthday month.

Girls

January	Calico
February	Lady
March	Countess
April	Mad
May	Madame
June	Mistress
July	Red
August	Shriekin'
September	Sleepy
October	Dirty
November	Skylarkin'
December	Buccaneer

Boys

January	Black
February	Captain
March	Count
April	Red
May	Sir
June	Mad
July	Bloody
August	Smugglin'
September	Dirty
October	Lord
November	Peg leg
December	Bald

First Names

Use the first letter of your first name to find your pirate first name.

Girls

A	Scarlett
B	Fleur
C	Esmerelda
D	Blanca
E	Rose
F	Indigo
G	Carlotta
H	Eliza
I	Bonney
J	Honor
K	Delight
L	Jane
M	Dixie
N	Prudence
O	London
P	Charity
Q	Renown
R	Grace
S	Constance
T	Hippolyta
U	Flame
V	Araby
W	Sabra
X	Molly
Y	Defiant
Z	Ariel

Boys

A	Nathaniel
B	Obadiah
C	Archibald
D	Shadrach
E	Jeremiah
F	Johnny
G	Isaiah
H	William
I	Solomon
J	Bartholomew
K	Royal
L	Defiance
M	Implacable
N	Caesar
O	Emilio
P	Phineas
Q	Bull
R	Hugo
S	Brewster
T	Jack
U	Sussex
V	Diabolito
W	Henry
X	Threepenny
Y	John Paul
Z	Xavier

Last Names

Use the first letter of your last name to find your pirate last name.

A	Mullett
B	Buckthorn
C	Buckler
D	Bonnet
E	Crickshank
F	Castle
G	Smythe
H	Quelch
I	Bellamy

J	Folkes
K	Crown
L	Wiggish
M	Foot
N	Canker
O	Truelove
P	Goodfellow
Q	Pintle
R	Hand
S	Brilliant
T	Fowler
U	Horngold
V	Tunny
W	Speedwell
X	Halifax
Y	Yanky
Z	Stede

• • • • • • •

Video Game Character Name

All the best ones are not taken yet! Find out yours using the list below.

First Names
Use your first initial to get the first name.

Girls
A	Ultra
B	Sky
C	Sister
D	Violet
E	Shatter
F	She
G	Rainbow
H	Purple
I	Moon
J	Astra
K	Micra
L	Aqua
M	Dark
N	Emerald
O	Electra
P	Future
Q	Lady
R	Phantom
S	Storm
T	Princess
U	Nova
V	Nimbus
W	Lightning
X	Starlight
Y	Fire
Z	Golden

Boys
A	Shield
B	Rocket
C	Samurai
D	Specter
E	Robot
F	Scout
G	Ninja
H	Master
I	Justice
J	Fury
K	Jet
L	Fire
M	Iron
N	Falcon
O	Eagle
P	Flame
Q	Demon
R	Blaze
S	Night
T	Cyber
U	Flying
V	Winged
W	He
X	Future
Y	Mega
Z	Magna

Last Names
Use your last initial to get the last name.

A	Titan
B	Ranger
C	Sword
D	Surfer
E	Ghost
F	Slayer
G	Spear
H	Racer
I	Avenger
J	Comet
K	Dragon
L	One
M	Rider
N	Ranger
O	Rider
P	Panther
Q	Vision
R	Warrior
S	Wolf
T	Singer
U	Hawk
V	Shadow
W	Emperor/Empress
X	Machine
Y	Hammer
Z	Ray

Undersea Explorer's Journal

You're an oceanographer who has just recorded these important discoveries in your journal. Now draw what they look like.

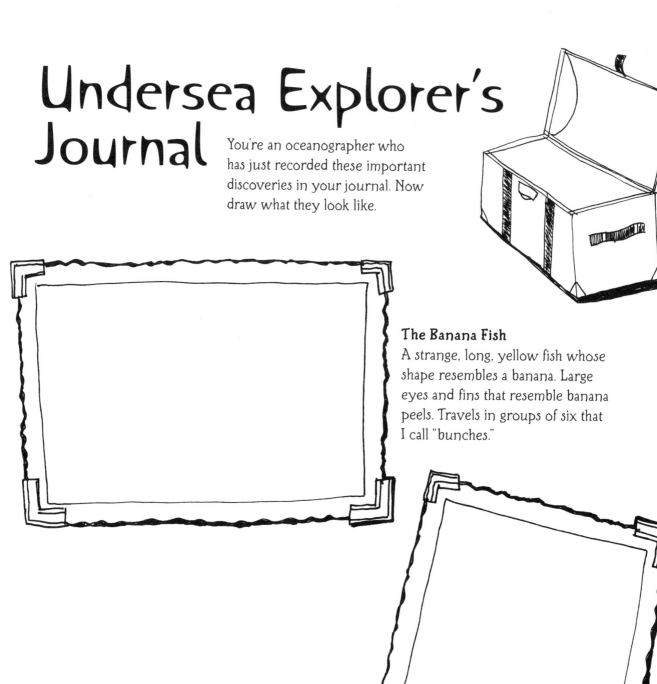

The Banana Fish
A strange, long, yellow fish whose shape resembles a banana. Large eyes and fins that resemble banana peels. Travels in groups of six that I call "bunches."

The Bat Shark
A shark with small beady eyes, pointy ears, and wing-like fins on the side. It has a funny turned-up snout and some very sharp fangs.

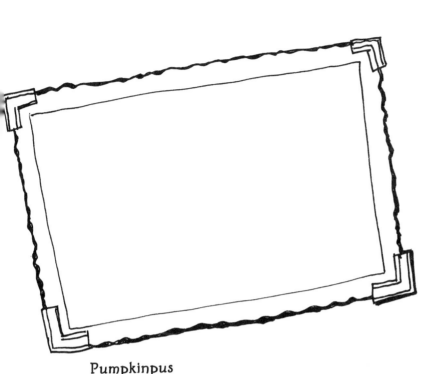

Pumpkinpus

A type of bright orange octopus with a rounded body and a stem growing out of the top of its head.

What else did you discover?

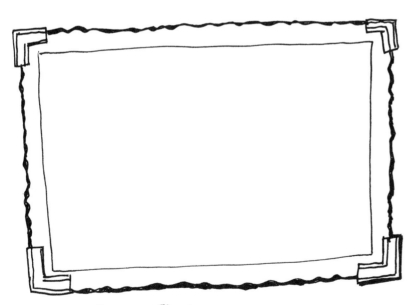

Treasure Chest

I found this sunken treasure chest, too. Can you believe all this stuff was in it?

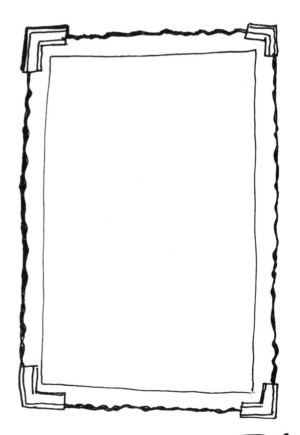

Codecracker

A challenging blend of skill and luck, this game will give your brain a little jog when it has been on autopilot for a little too long.

How to Play

- The first player thinks of a four-digit code. It can be any combination of numbers between 1 and 8.

- The player writes this code on a slip of paper and keeps it hidden from the second player.

- The second player guesses at the code, writing his guess in the bottom row of a grid.

- The first player looks at the guess and marks the correct numbers with a star and the wrong ones with an x. Each number not only has to be correct, but it has to be in the correct order.

- Using that information, the second player guesses again, writing a new guess in the next row of the grid, moving up. Again, the first player marks correct numbers with a star and wrong ones with an x.

- The second player continues guessing. If he gets all the numbers right by the time he reaches the top row, he wins. If not, the code creator wins.

- You could also play this game using two grids at a time, each player alternating between guessing and marking the other player's guesses.

- If you want more hints, the code creator can circle numbers that are correct but in the wrong place. Or, she can provide a greater-than or less-than sign for wrong numbers one time each round when the guesser asks for it.

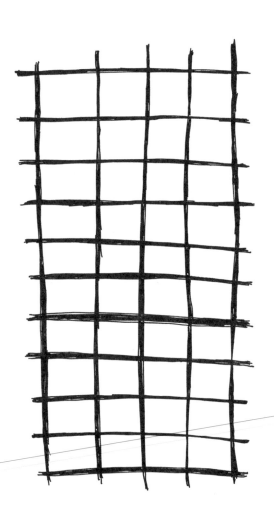

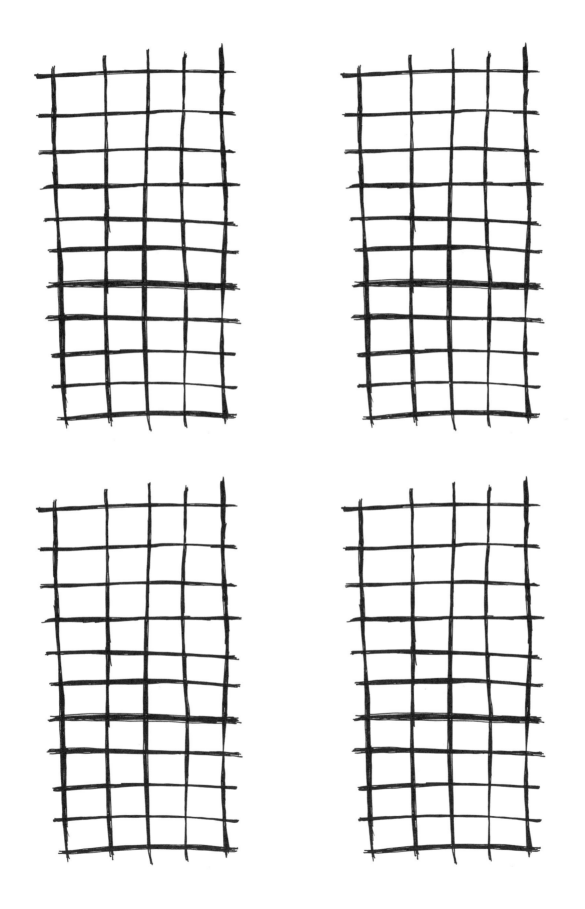

The Tattoo Man

The tattoo man from the circus is famous for his 20 tattoos.
Can you copy all of them onto him?

Don't forget to decorate the
Tattoo Man's little sister, Lulu.

Sprouts

Challenge one of your travel partners to a game of sprouts. All you need is a pencil and some time on your hands. (You've got that, right?) You can use the boxes on the opposite page to play nine games. When you've got Sprouts down, move on to Brussels Sprouts on the following pages.

How to Play

- Draw two or more dots in one of the boxes on the opposite page (step 1). The more dots you start off with, the longer the game lasts. They can be anywhere and don't necessarily need to be near each other.

- The first player draws a line connecting two dots or from one dot to itself. Then the player adds a new dot to the midpoint of the line she drew (step 2). The next player draws another line connecting two dots. The only rule about the line is that it can't cross any other line. Then the player adds a dot to his line (step 3).

- A dot with three lines connected to it (counting a loop from a spot to itself as two lines) is "dead" and may not have any more lines connected to it. Can you find the three dead dots in step 4? How many dead dots do you see in step 5?

- The game ends when there are no more live dots to connect to or there's no way to connect any live dots. The last player to make a move wins (step 6).

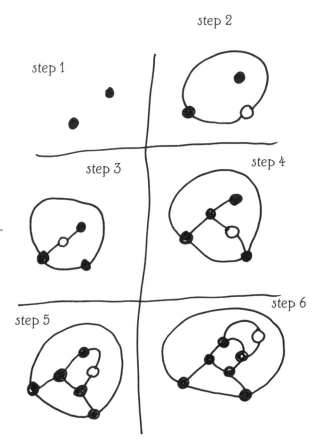

step 1

step 2

step 3

step 4

step 5

step 6

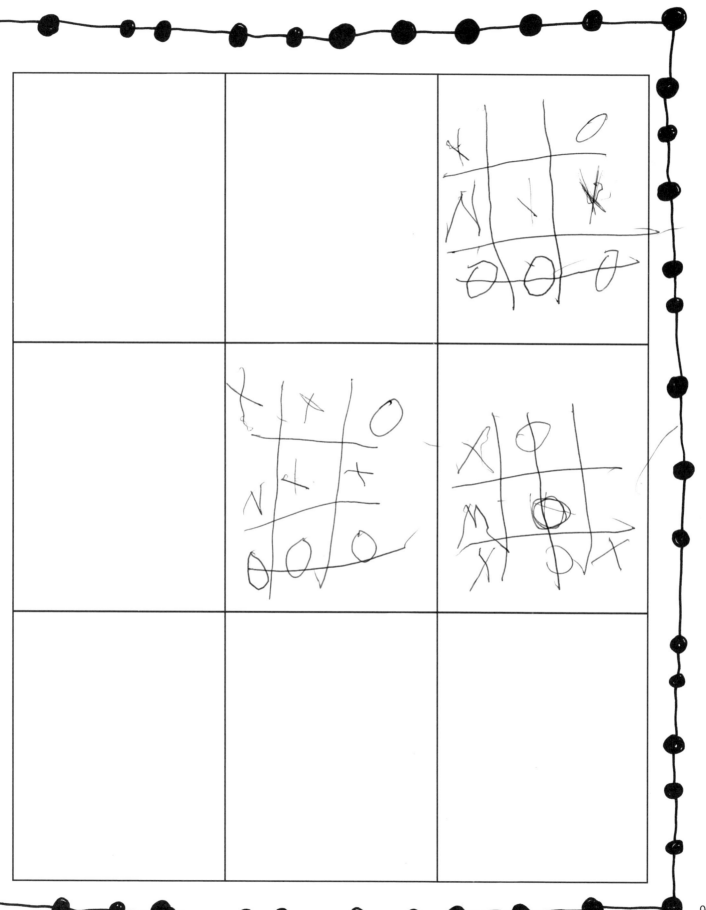

Brussels Sprouts

This game is a lot like Sprouts, but it's different, too.

Start with a number of crosses (lines with four free ends). To make a move, a player joins two free ends with a curvy line (again, not crossing an existing line), and then draws a short stroke across the line. Each move removes two free ends from a pair of crosses and introduces two more. The game is over when the ends of the crosses can no longer be connected without crossing a line.

For example:

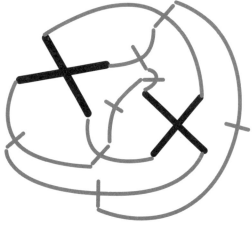

Here are some crosses to get you started:

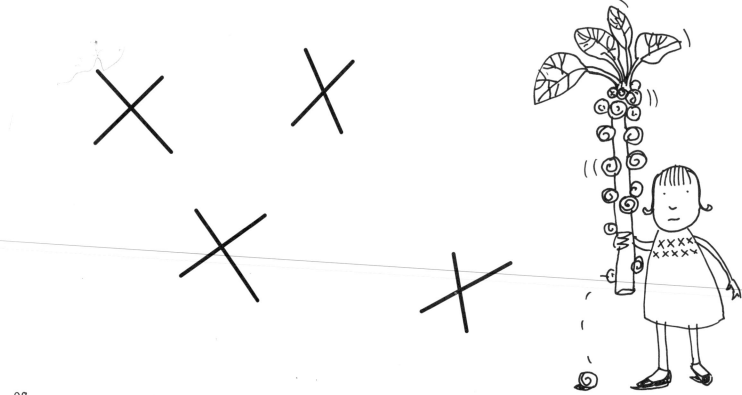

Here are more boxes so you can play either Sprouts game!

Draw These Animals

Snack Attack

Under ordinary circumstances, your parents would probably tell you not to play with your food. But when you're trying to pass the time on a long trip, all bets are off. Here are some quick time killers that will keep you amused for minutes at a time.

Potato Chips

Get the baked kind. They're easier to work with—and healthier.

- Place two potato chips in your mouth, one with the curve facing up and one with the curve facing down. Instant duck bill! (Amusement time: at least 30 seconds.)

- When you get to your refueling station, get several different types of chips (four or five if possible). Remove one or more of the chips from its bag and have your travel partner close her eyes or wear a blindfold of sorts. Perform a taste test! Give your partner one chip at a time and have her guess the brand. (Amusement time: at least five minutes.)

- Add chips between layers of your sandwich for extra crunch. (Amusement time: all through lunch.)

Oranges

- Put an orange slice in your mouth (with the skin still on it) so that it looks like it's your teeth. (Amusement time: about 20 seconds, unless it gets stuck in there.)

- Squeeze the juice into a cup and see how much you get (a napkin close by is required.) (Amusement time: several minutes.)

- Try to make a picture out of the peel! (Amusement time: a long time.)

Apples

- Start saying the alphabet as you twist the stem. Whichever letter you say just as it snaps off is supposed to be the first initial of your true love. Now poke at the apple with the stem while saying the alphabet. The letter you're saying when you pierce the skin is the second initial of your true love. (Amusement time: at least a minute.)

- Try to tie a knot in the stem. (Amusement time: a frustrating 20 minutes, at least.)

- See who can balance an apple on his head for the longest time. (Amusement time: this could go on for a long time.)

Pretzels

Get pretzel sticks rather than the traditional shape—they're more fun to play with!

- Try to arrange the sticks into a picture. (Amusement time: as long as you want.)

- If you have cookies and/or a tiny round snack, such as raisins, make spiders! This could be a good excuse to ask your parents to buy you some cookies. (Amusement time: at least 20 minutes).

- Try to write your name in pretzels. (Amusement time: a good three minutes.)

French Fries

- Stick two in your mouth to make walrus tusks. (Amusement time: mere seconds.)

- Play NIM on page 161. (Amusement time: up to five minutes.)

- Don't stick them in your nose or ears...that's just gross.

Candy

- Hold a candy rally. You'll need round, hard candy—preferably the kind with holes in the center. Find a hard surface and a starting line. You and your opponent each place a candy on its side at the starting line. Roll your candies at the same time. See whose candy rolls the farthest before falling down. (Amusement time: a couple minutes max.)

Graffiti Artist

Don't do this in real life! But in this book, you can cover the urban landscape with graffiti!

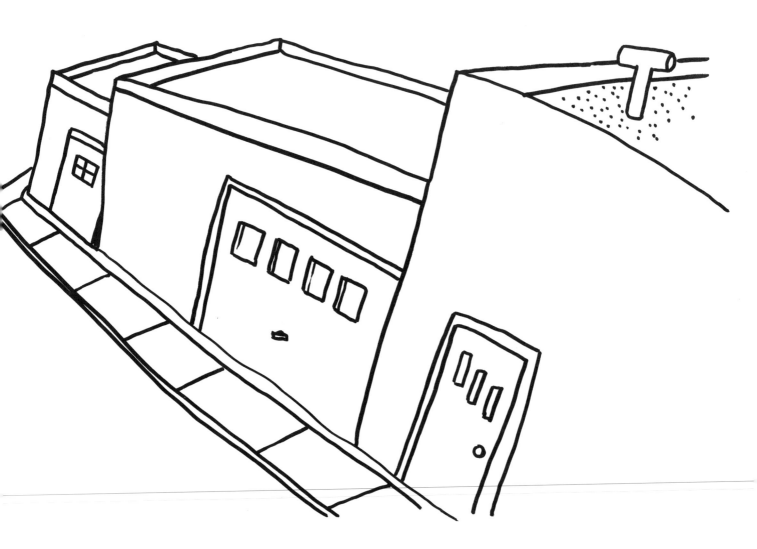

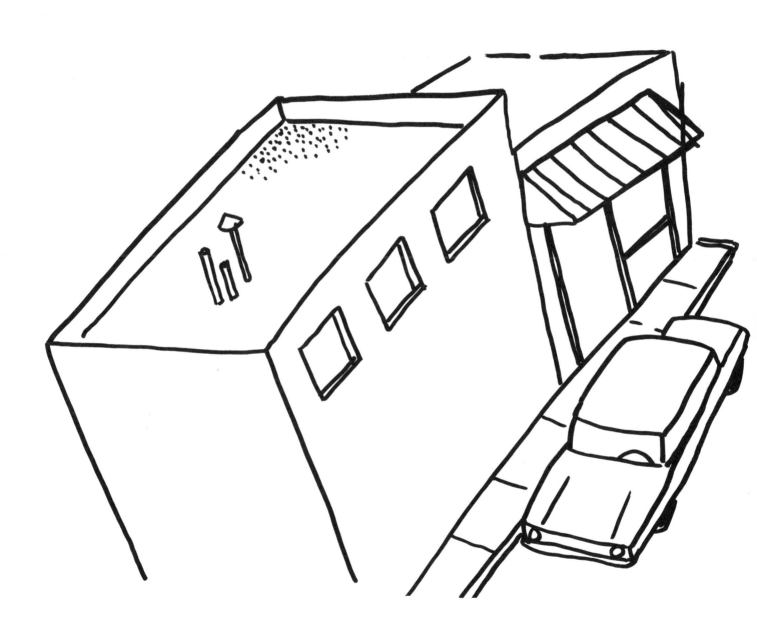

Do You Sudoku?

Sudoku is a number-placing puzzle based on a 9 x 9 grid containing several given numbers. The object is to place numbers in the empty squares so that each row, each column, and each 3 x 3 box contains the numbers 1 to 9 only once.

Example 1

	a	b	c	d	e	f
1	2		4			6
2		1				
3	3		5	2		
4			6	3		5
5					2	
6	4			5		3

Example 2

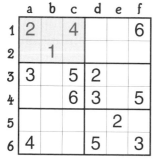

	a	b	c	d	e	f
1	2		4			6
2	6	1				
3	3		5	2		
4			6	3		5
5					2	
6	4			5		3

Example 3

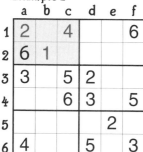

	a	b	c	d	e	f
1	2		4			6
2	6	1				
3	3		5	2		
4		2	6	3		5
5					2	
6	4			5		3

Example 4

	a	b	c	d	e	f
1	2	X	4	X	X	6
2	6	1	X	X	X	
3	3	X	5	2	X	X
4	X	2	6	3	X	5
5	X	X	X	X	2	X
6	4	X		5	X	3

The easiest way to begin solving a Sudoku puzzle is to start in boxes (outlined in bold) that already have lots of numbers. In Example 1 (an easier 6 x 6 grid that uses the numbers 1 to 6), box 1 (gray area) already has 2, 1, and 4. All it needs is a 3, 5, and 6. The number 6 can only go in square 2A since there's already a 6 in row 1 and there's also a 6 in column C (Example 2). Can you fill in any more numbers in box 1? How about the other boxes?

Another way to fill in squares is to scan rows and columns, looking for numbers that can and won't fit. Keep your eyes open for situations where only one number can fit in a single square. In Example 2, row 4 already has 6, 3, and 5. So it only needs 1, 2, and 4. Try to fill in the number 2. It can't go in square 4A since there's a 2 already in column A. It also can't go in square 4E since there's a 2 in column E AND there's a 2 in box 4. The only square available to you is 4B (Example 3).

In fact, look at all the places where you can't put a 2 (Example 4). You can fill in the rest of your 2s.

See if you can solve the rest of this puzzle.

	a	b	c	d	e	f
1	2		4			6
2	6	1				2
3	3		5	2		
4		2	6	3		5
5					2	
6	4		2	5		3

Example

We've provided you with several sudoku puzzles on the next three pages. Start with the easy 4 x 4 grids and work your way up to the 9 x 9s. The answers are on page 248. Good luck!

Puzzle 1

4			
	3		1
1		2	
			4

Puzzle 2

	3		4
4	2		
		4	2
2		1	

Puzzle 3

		6	5		
	4			1	
6					5
1					2
	5			6	
		3	2		

Puzzle 4

5	6		2	1	
2					4
					5
4					
6					1
	5	3		4	2

Puzzle 5

		2			4
	5				
6		4			
			6		1
				6	
3			5		

Puzzle 6

4	2				
				6	4
6	4				
				4	1
3	6				
				5	6

Puzzle 7

	6	4	1	3	
	1			6	
	4			2	
	3	1	5	4	

Puzzle 8

	5	6			
		3	5	2	
1					
					4
	4	5	1		
			4	6	

Puzzle 9

		3	7		8	1		
	2		5				9	
5	6	1	9			7	4	8
8				3		5	2	7
				1				
6	4	5		7				3
2	3	4			7	6	8	5
	5				4		7	
		7	6		2	9		

Puzzle 10

		4	1	2	9		7	
	8	3						
7		2	6			9	4	
4				8			6	1
1	6		4		7		3	9
2	3		9					8
	7	1			5	6		2
						3	1	
	2		7	9	1	5		

Puzzle 11

	4	6	9		7	8	3	
			5		6			
	2	5				6	7	
9	1			3			8	6
			4		9			
5	7			6			9	1
	9	7				3	1	
			3		4			
	5	2	8		1	9	6	

Puzzle 12

	7							
		8		2	7	6		1
	6			8	1		4	
	9	3	7		2			
	4	7				3	5	
			9		4	2	7	
	1		5	7			3	
5		9	8	1		7		
							8	

Puzzle 13

		2	8	7	1	6		
	1		5		3		8	
		4				1		
5	7						1	2
2				5				8
3	8						5	7
		3				7		
	2		9		6		4	
		8	4	3	7	5		

Puzzle 14

			3			7		
		8	6			3		2
	6	3	1	4		5		
	4	6			1			
1		9				5		8
			2			4	9	
	3			1	6	9	8	
7		4			9	1		
	9			8				

Puzzle 15

					4		9	
	9		7			3	1	
			1	8			7	
9		3			6			8
6			5			1		2
	6			2	3			
	5	4			7		6	
	7		9					

Puzzle 16

	4	7	2			5	3	
	1		5				8	
		8	1			7		
						9	1	7
3	5	6						
		2		1		8		
	7			3			4	
	8	9		5		1	6	

Puzzle 17

			1	4	9			
		6		7		9		
	9					8		
9			2		1			7
1	4						3	6
8			4		6			5
	7					5		
		1		2		4		
			5	9	4			

Puzzle 18

		2	9		6	3		
			5	3	4			
		1				9		
6	7						3	8
	2			5			9	
1	9						2	7
		9				4		
			3	4	2			
			6	8		7	2	

Achi

Just say no to tic-tac-toe—try Achi instead. Achi is a game from Ghana, a country on the west coast of Africa. The game requires a little more strategy than tic-tac-toe, and once you've got the hang of it, it's a lot more fun.

I want to play ACHI!

Gesundheit.

How to Play

• You'll need two players.

• Each of you has three tokens. You can use coins in different denominations, or any other small object that will fit on the board. (Just make sure each player has three pieces that are similar to each other, but different from those of the other player.)

• Like tic-tac-toe, the object of Achi is to get three of your tokens in a row, and to prevent your opponent from doing so.

• Use the board on the opposite page.

• Decide who goes first.

• Players take turns placing one token at a time on the dots on the board.

• If neither player has achieved three in a row after all tokens are on the board, each takes a turn sliding a token along a line to an empty dot. Jumping over pieces is against the rules.

• The winner is the first player to have all three pieces in a row. If you want to make the game more challenging, agree that one of the pieces in your row must be in the center dot of the board.

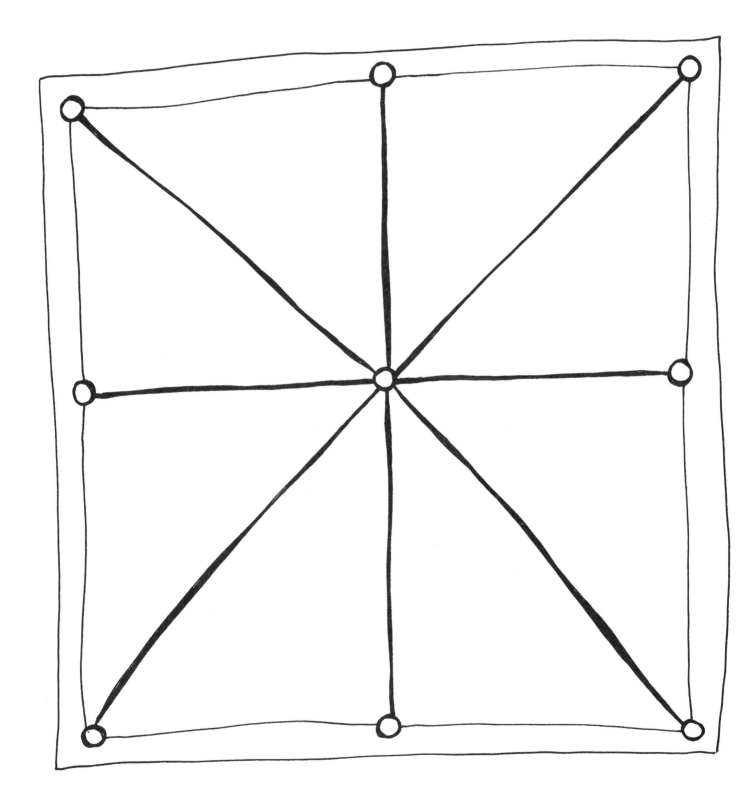

Surf's Up

Surf's up. Add surfers.

Decorate these surfboards.

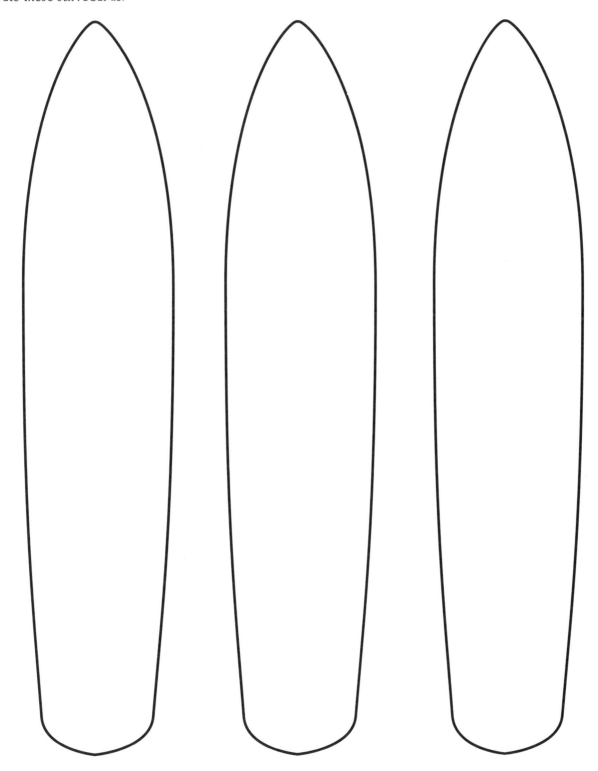

Something's Secret

All of these games have rules, but they're secret—at least to some of the players. How do you discover the rules? That's the fun of playing the games.

Plane Trip

This game requires at least two players, but it's more fun with three or more. Each player will say, "I'm going to take a plane to...," but only one player—the secret-keeper—knows what must be true for the other players to arrive at their destination successfully.

- Each player takes a turn as the secret-keeper.

- The first secret-keeper chooses a rule. Let's say the first rule is that the players must choose a place in Africa.

- The first person says, "I'm going to take a plane to London." The secret keeper will tell the person, "You didn't get there." But if the next player says, "I'm going to take a plane to Nairobi," the secret keeper will say, "You got there." Play continues with everyone guessing until each has given an answer, which demonstrates an understanding of the secret.

- Secret-keepers can pick tricky secrets, such as "a city that's really rainy" or "a place that begins with the letter L."

- The secret doesn't have to be in the name of the place. Instead, it could be in the way the sentence is said. For example, it could be that the players need to hesitate and to use an expression such as "um" or "uh" before saying the name of the place. In other words, "I'm going to take a plane to Tokyo" won't get the player there, but "I'm going to take a plane to...um...Tokyo" will.

The Green Glass Door

What's behind the Green Glass Door? You know, but your fellow players don't. The "secret" that you know is that everything behind the green glass door is spelled with two double letters (green glass door). This game can only be played with people who have never played it before (otherwise, they'll know the secret).

Here are some examples of clues that you can give to the other players to help them guess:

- Flowers may bloom there but they don't grow there.

- There are books but no shelves.

- There is a moon but no sun.

- There are streets but no roads.

- There are pools but no water.

- There are feet but no shoes.

- There are wheels but no cars.

- The reverse of this game is known as "The Red Plastic Window," in which there are no objects spelled with double letters. For example, there are animals but no sheep.

Paradise Island

- For this game, you'll need four or more players. Two of the players will know the "secret," while the others won't. They'll try to guess. When they've figured it out, the game is over.

- A leader for the game is chosen. The leader chooses the secret that answers the question: What kind of things can be taken to Paradise Island? For example, the leader might decide that only things made out of wood can be taken along. The leader lets one player know the secret.

- The player who knows the secret starts the game by giving a clue to the others in the form of a sentence like: "I'm going to Paradise Island. I can take a tree, but not a leaf." The clue has to include one thing that can be taken and one that can't.

- Based on the clue, the next player has to guess. No one confirms that the guess is correct or incorrect, but the leader continues to provide clues until it is obvious that all the players have finally caught onto the secret.

Totem Poles

Doodle some totem poles.

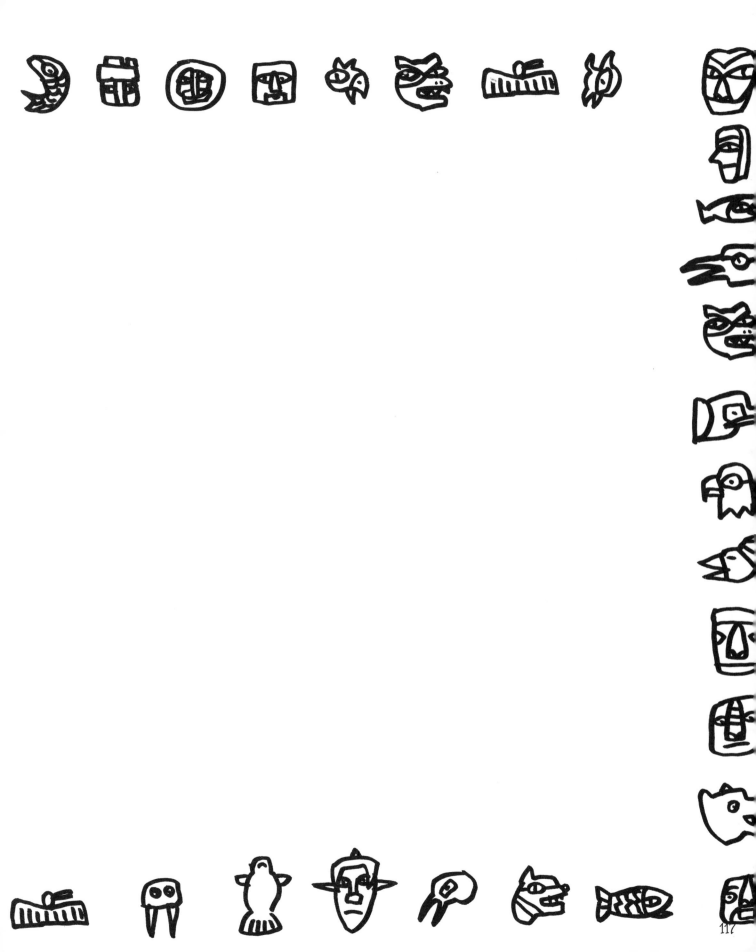

Talk with Your Hands

If you're going to talk with your hands, be articulate. Knowing sign language is a great communication skill to have. You might get carsick before you're fluent, but at least learn to spell your name or sign a secret message.

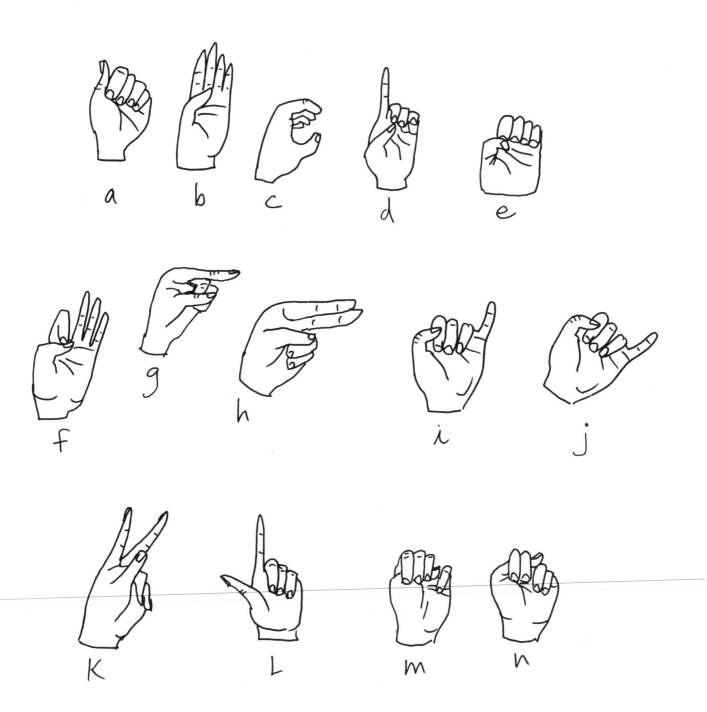

o

p

q

r

s

t

u

v

w

x

y

z

Yo!

The First Annual Cosmic Convergence

Aliens from all over the galaxy have gathered for the first time in this Las Vegas convention center to get to know one another. Draw more delegates from different planets.

Who's having their picture taken with the Las Vegas showgirl?

Not Your Grandma's Sing-Along

It's one thing to know the words to "Home on the Range," but it's something completely different to come up with your own words. Making your travel partners memorize and sing along? That's just mean.

Here's how:

- *Use the same number of syllables in your substitute as the words you replace, and your remix should work.*

- *While you sing, purse your lips and hold your nose to make your voice sound funny. Need percussion? Use your knuckles to knock on a window, beat on your the car seat, and stamp on the floor.*

- *Sing, "We left Billy at the rest stop/Did you know!?" to the tune of "She'll Be Coming 'Round the Mountain."*

Keep the tunes coming by changing the words to these songs:

- Twinkle, Twinkle Little Star
- Give My Regards to Broadway
- Any Beatles' song

- Blowing in the Wind
- America, the Beautiful
- The Brady Bunch Theme Song

- Yankee Doodle
- Dixie
- It's a Small World, After All
- Amazing Grace
- When the Saints Go Marching In
- Big Rock Candy Mountain
- B-I-N-G-O
- Do Re Mi
- My Favorite Things
- For He's a Jolly Good Fellow
- (How Much Is That) Doggie in the Window?
- I've Been Workin' on the Railroad
- Wild Thing
- Michael, Row Your Boat Ashore
- Oh, What a Beautiful Morning
- Take Me Out to the Ball Game
- Wheels on the Bus

You can also try this with Nursery Rhymes

Drive, drive, drive the van

Gently down the street.

Merrily, merrily, merrily, merrily

When can we stop to eat?

Write your masterpieces here:

_____

_____

_____

_____

_____

_____

_____

_____

_____

Wish You Were Here

Going away is great, but sometimes you can find yourself missing someone you left behind. So, why not drop him a line? Design your own postcard here. Write a message in the space on the opposite page.

Design the front of the card here:

Write your message here.
Don't forget to design a
stamp, too!

PL8S

Decipher these vanity license plates. See answers on page 249.

2TH DR

_____

1DFUL

_____

YRUNVS

_____

B GR8

_____

2Z RES-Q

_____

I8CFOOD

_____

O2BNLA

_____

2M8O

_____

L8 4 A D8

_____

I XLR8

ICUNIYQ

_____

_____

IMZ14U

IBCNU

_____

_____

2 BZ 4 U

YY 4U

_____

Cre8 your own:

IM4 PZ RU

_____

_____

ICU RUOK

_____

_____

Portrait of a Traveler

On these pages, draw portraits of those traveling with you. When you're done, ask everyone else to guess who each person is. If you're a really good artist and you're sure everyone will guess correctly, try making your drawing a little abstract to make things more interesting.

Landmark Lotto!

You know **what** it is (probably). But **where** is it? Take this quiz to see how much you know. Answers on page 249.

North America

1. What is it? _____
   Where is it?
   A. Wyoming
   B. Colorado
   C. California
   D. South Dakota

2. What is it? _____
   Where is it?
   A. Chicago
   B. St. Louis
   C. Dallas
   D. Miami

3. What is it? _____
   Where is it?
   A. Seattle
   B. Las Vegas
   C. San Francisco
   D. Vancouver

4. What is it? _____
   Where is it?
   A. New York City
   B. Brooklyn
   C. Boston
   D. Los Angeles

5. What is it? _____
   Where is it?
   A. Minnesota
   B. Indiana
   C. Georgia
   D. South Dakota

The World!

1. What is it? _____
   Where is it?
   A. Agra, India
   B. Tokyo, Japan
   C. Bangkok, Thailand
   D. Mecca, Saudi Arabia

3. What is it? _____
   Where is it?
   A. London, England
   B. Paris, France
   C. Edinburgh, Scotland
   D. Madrid, Spain

4. What is it? _____
   Where is it?
   A. Giza, Egypt
   B. Athens, Greece
   C. Rome, Italy
   D. Cairo, Egypt

2. What is it? _____
   Where is it?
   A. Paris, France
   B. Moscow, Russia
   C. Rome, Italy
   D. Geneva, Switzerland

5. What is it? _____
   Where is it?
   A. Scotland
   B. England
   C. China
   D. Japan

Whose Shoes?

Draw the owners of these wonderful shoes.

Place Name Scavenger Hunt

Are you up for another scavenger hunt? This time you'll be collecting the interesting place names you pass. Your journey may take you to New London or Old Town, Whale Harbor or Deer Creek, or even to places with crazy names like Pigtown or Boring. If you're going on a short trip, or if you just like map reading, try this game using a map or atlas.

A place with a color in its name (Greenville, Brownsville) _____

A place with an animal in its name (Moosehead Lake, Deer Run, Bear Creek) _____

_____

A place with a Native American/aboriginal name (Chattahoochee, Saskatoon, Ogunquit) _____

_____

A place name taken from another language (Des Moines, Lafayette, Santa Clara) _____

_____

A place named after a famous person (Washington, Austin, Prince Edward Island) _____

_____

A place named after another place (New London, New Braunfels, Paris, Dublin) _____

_____

A street with a funny name _____

A street/road with a number name _____

A place with a size in its name (Little Switzerland, Big Creek) _____

A place named after a concept (Hope, Prosperity, Welcome, Harmony, Progress) _____

_____

A place with a direction in its name (North, South, East, West) _____

A place with a strange name (Kickapoo, Cow's Lick, Big Ugly, Fear Not) _____

_____

A street named after a famous person (Martin Luther King Drive, Ave Cartier) _____

_____

A business with a funny name (Firework Palace, House of Lawn Furniture) _____

_____

A place with "ville" in its name _____

A place with "town or ton" in its name _____

A place name with a purpose (name includes Harbor, Port, Landing, Junction, Fields, Ferry, Bridge, etc.)

_____

A place with a plant or tree name (Pine Ridge, Daisy Hill, Magnolia)_____

_____

A place named for a topographic feature (Mountain, Hill, River, Lake, Falls)_____

_____

Have You Been To...?

Eek, Alaska

Hairy Hills, Alberta

Head-Smashed-In-Buffalo-Jump, Alberta

Goobertown, Arizona

Toadsuck, Arkansas

Oddville, Kentucky

Slickpoo, Idaho

Accident, Maryland

Tightwad, Missouri

Wahoo, Nebraska

Blow-Me-Down, Newfoundland

Hell Hollow, New Hampshire

Boogertown, North Carolina

Heart's Content, Nova Scotia

Okay, Oklahoma

Punkeydoodles Corners, Ontario

St. Louis-du-Ha! Ha!, Quebec

Imalone, Wisconsin

Funny Faces

Can you draw what these faces would look like?

Has just seen a tarantula on his shoulder

Spent the night in a wet sleeping bag

Is sprouting hair in unlikely places

Pet lizard just ran away

Was just voted "Most Amazing Kid in the World"

Has just realized shirt is on inside out at school assembly

Has just discovered that thing floating in the pool is not a candy bar

License Plate Games

What's flat, multicolored, and has lots of pictures and letters you can do things with? No, not your computer screen. Look out the window.

License Plate Whiz

What to Do

1. Take turns. When it's your turn, quickly add up the numbers on the plate of the car passing. Ignore any letters.

2. When it's your turn again, add the total from the new plate to your previous total.

3. When a player reaches 100 points or more, finish the round so everyone's had an equal number of turns. Add up your scores. Highest score wins.

License Plate Alphabet

Find A through Z, in order, on the plates of the cars you pass. If you forget where you are, you have to start over.

License Plate Story

1. Working in order of the cars you pass, each player should write down the letters and numbers of a plate, also noting its state and any decorations on the plate.

2. When everyone's ready, take turns making up a story based on your notes. You can come up with more rules as you play.

"A" Stands for...

1. Each player goes in order, writing down the first license plate he spots when it's his turn. Write the numbers and letters across the page, leaving as much space between them as you can.

2. For 15 minutes, watch out the window for things whose names begin with a letter you saw on the plate. Write them down in columns under their matching letters. Also look for things in groups that match the numbers on the plate. If a plate had the number 11, it's okay to look for one each of two different things. Your goal is to find as many things as you can for each number and letter. Each item you spot is worth a point.

3. At the end of 15 minutes, everyone should total up his items. Highest scorer wins.

Top Spotter Bingo

Keep an eye peeled for special digit and number combinations, and you can win!

1. Every player gets her own blank copy of the Logo Bingo grid. Rip out the ones below or make your own with the blank pages at the back of this book.

2. Have an adult call out random two-digit numbers and double letter combinations (26, 33, AD, HH, for example). Going in a circle, take turns writing down what's called out until everyone's filled in their grids.

3. Now, the hunt starts! As players find matches on license plates for sections of their bingo cards, they should call them out and cross them off. First person to cross off everything on the card wins and gets to yell, Bingo!

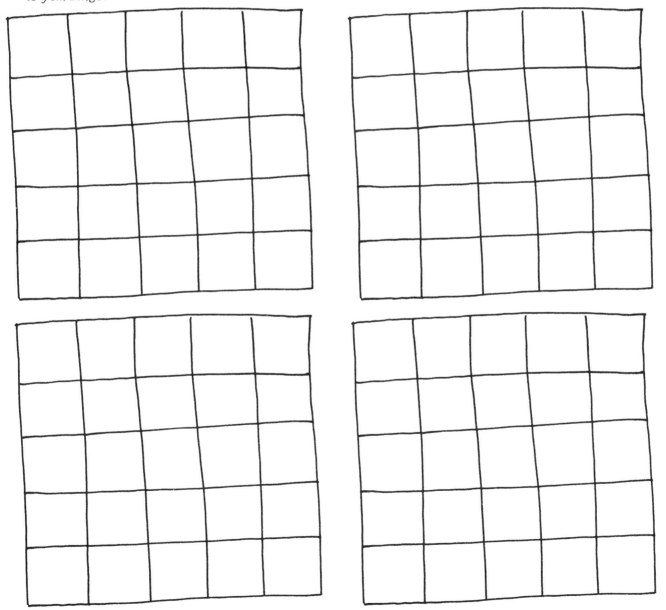

A Little Shut-Eye

Relax. Close your eyes. But don't go to sleep. There are plenty of games you can play with your eyes shut.

What's Changed?

This game challenges your power of observation. Have your partner look carefully at you and try to memorize the details of your appearance. Your partner should then close her eyes. Change something—if your collar was down, put it up; arrange your hair differently; unbutton a button; take off a bracelet. When you're done, tell your partner to open her eyes. See if she can guess what changed.

Time Flies

For this one, you'll need a watch with a second hand or some other accurate time-keeping device. Check the time. Just as a new minute starts, you and your partner should close your eyes. When you think a minute has passed, open them. See how close you can get to guessing the right time. You'll be surprised how long a minute can feel!

Blindfolded Quick Pics

For this game you'll need three people, scraps of paper, and something to use as a blindfold. One person writes down a word on a scrap of paper and shows it to the person who will be the "artist." The artist will then try to draw the object on scrap paper—while blindfolded! (Use the blank page opposite.) The third person tries to guess what the artist is drawing.

Draw your masterpiece here.

Just Improvise!

Are you good at thinking on your feet, or in this case, in your seat? Just because you can't move around much in the car or plane doesn't mean you can't exercise your quick wit and verbal agility. These games were developed to help actors practice improv comedy, in which they were expected to invent their lines and performances on the spot. The games take some time to get good at, so try a few, learn some tricks, and then try them again later.

Gibberish

Two players are needed for this game. One player is the gibberish speaker. The other has to "translate" the gibberish and do what the gibberish speaker asks. For example, the gibberish speaker might want to tell the other player to roll down her window. He would make up completely unidentifiable words for the action. Consistency is important. The word for window has to be the same each time it's repeated. The gibberish speaker can use hand gestures as well. The game ends when the player successfully figures out what it is she's being asked to do.

What's the Question?

This game is similar to the TV quiz show "Jeopardy." The group brainstorms words that are answers, such as "yellow," "at midnight," "in the jungle," "with your eyes closed," "100 pounds," or "at the end of the school year." The moderator gives each player an answer, and the player comes up with a funny question for it. For example, if the answer was "dog food," the question could be: "What is the main ingredient in the world's best birthday cake?" Like "Jeopardy," players are given a time limit for coming up with a question.

60-Second Alphabet

This game requires two players. The players pretend to have a conversation, but it's guided by this rule: each sentence must start with a different letter of the alphabet, in consecutive order. For example:

"**A**manda, have you met my friend Betty?"

"**B**etty?"

"**C**ertainly, Betty."

"**D**on't know if I have..."

"**E**verybody loves Betty..."

"**F**or sure..."

The scene continues either until the entire alphabet is used or the conversation hits a point when it doesn't make sense anymore.

Aa Bb Cc Dd Ee Ff Gg Hh Ii Jj Kk Ll Mm Nn Oo Pp Qq Rr Ss Tt Uu Vv Ww Xx Yy Zz

Ask the Expert

This game features two panelists who question an expert. The panelists secretly agree on a topic. (Some topics the expert might know about are surfing, dinosaurs, aliens, chocolate, soccer, etc.) The expert doesn't know what he's an expert in, and must guess based on the panelists' questions.

Mu Torere

The Maori people of New Zealand have been playing this strategy game for thousands of years. It's played on a star-shaped board like the one on the opposite page. The goal of the game is to move your pieces in such a way so that your opponent can't move his.

How to Play

- Each player gets four playing pieces in a single color. For game pieces, you can use coins or anything that's small and round or flat, as long as you have two different colors (one player could use raisins and the other peanuts, or you could use jellybeans or other kinds of candy). Be careful playing in the car or your pieces will move around.
- Play starts with the each player positioning his pieces on one half of the outer circle. For example, green jellybeans get the top star points and red get the bottom star points, or red get the right side and green the left.
- The player with the pieces of the darkest color goes first.
- The first move is always into the center.
- A piece may only move if one or both points next to it are occupied by the opponent's pieces. For example, a red jellybean can only move if there's a green jellybean next to it.
- After the first move, players take turns moving onto another star point or into the center—whatever space is open.
- Players cannot jump over an opponent's pieces.
- The winner is the one who successfully blocks the other player from making any more moves.
- No passing turns.
- Sounds simple, huh? Just give it a try. This game can sure make a long trip fly by.

Draw Faces

Using the blank page, draw heads like this!

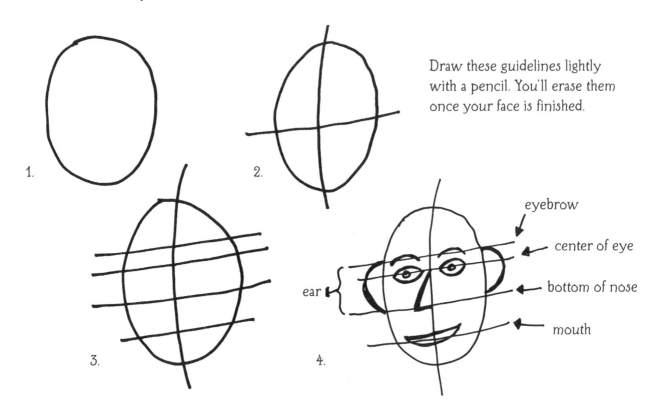

1.

2. Draw these guidelines lightly with a pencil. You'll erase them once your face is finished.

3.

4.
- eyebrow
- center of eye
- bottom of nose
- mouth
- ear

After you've drawn heads, put your choice of these features on them. Or create your own!

Origami Crane

1. To make your rectangular piece of paper square, follow illustrations 1 and 2 on page 42.

2. Fold the paper in half diagonally (ill. 1). Then, fold along the dotted line (ill. 2). Your paper should look like ill. 3.

3. Flip the triangle so the folded edges are at the top. Open the top flap (ill. 4), and flatten it to make a square (ill. 5 and 6).

4. Turn over (ill. 7) and repeat. Crease the folds well. You should have a square (ill. 8).

5. Flip the square so that the open corner is at the top. Fold the upper flaps along the dotted lines (ill. 9). Turn over and repeat (ill. 10).

6. Crease along the dotted line (ill. 11). Unfold all the main folds (ill. 12).

7. Bring the top upper flap down and fold along the crease (ill. 13).

8. Turn over and do the same thing (ill. 14). Your crane should look like ill. 15.

9. Turn the crane body over (ill. 16) and fold the flaps along the dotted lines (ill. 17). Turn over and repeat (ill. 18).

10. Open one of the side folds and bring the lower section up to the inside of the body, folding along the fold line and ultimately, reversing the fold (ill. 19). Repeat with the other side fold.

11. For the beak (ill. 20), open one tip, and then push in to flatten and reverse the fold. Open the wings (ill. 21).

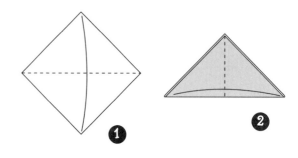

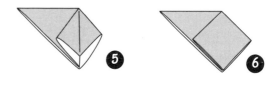

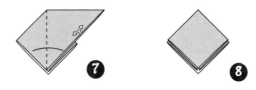

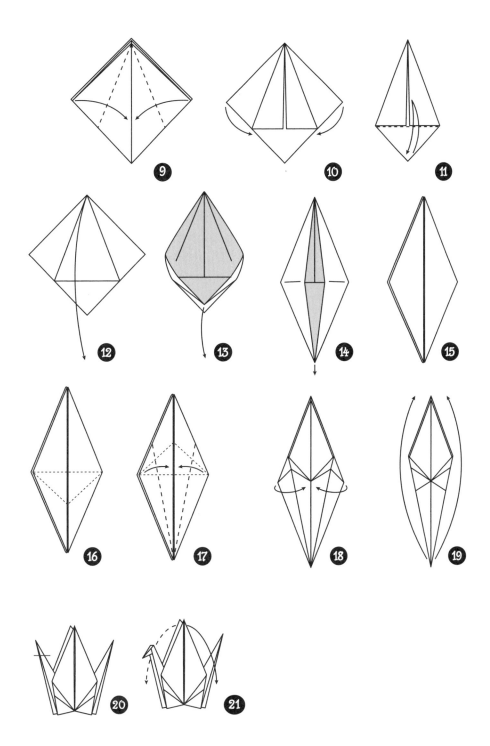

What's On Your Mind?

Long trips give you plenty of time to think, think, think. What are you thinking about now? What do you usually think about? Examine the examples below and then make your own mind map.

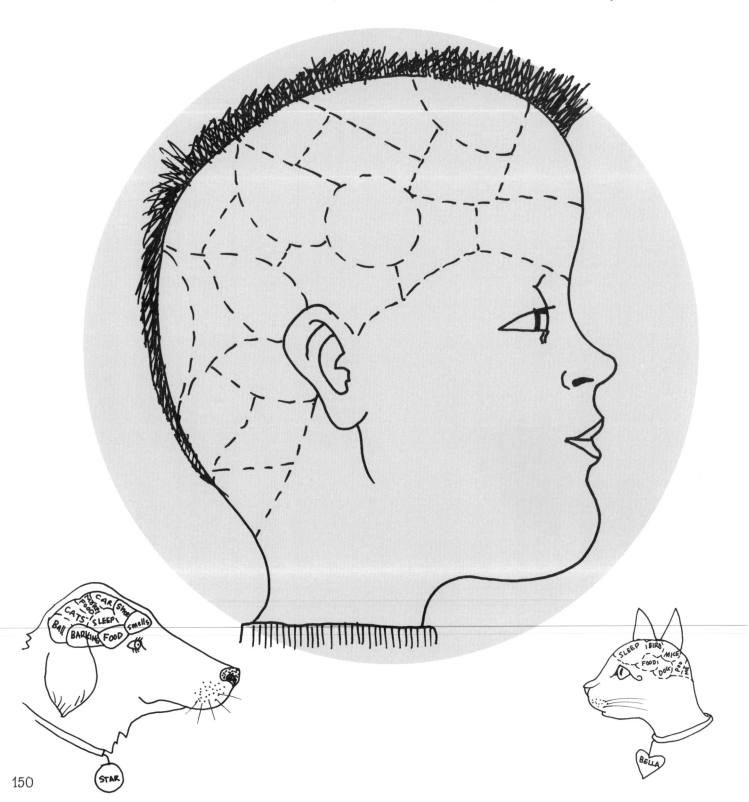

Who's in Charge?

The Left Brain Controls:	The Right Brain Controls:
Number skills	Insight
Written language	Three-dimensional thinking
Spoken language	Imagination
Scientific skills	Music awareness
Right-hand control	Art awareness
	Left-hand control

MYTH-BUSTER!

You may have heard that humans only use 10% of their brains. Not true! We can use 100% of our brains. Though some of it might not be used all the time, no part of your brain sits there for long periods of time and just twiddles its thumbs.

Brain Facts

Number of pounds the average adult brain weighs

Number of digits your working memory can hold at one time

100 billion

Number of brain cells you were born with

Trillions

Number of connections your brain will make before you grow up

Brain Freeze

How does brain freeze happen? When something really cold touches the center of your palate (on the roof of your mouth), the nerves in that area spasm (cramp) and tell your brain's blood vessels to get bigger. That's what causes the pain. Don't worry—your brain will not actually freeze and there won't be any permanent damage. Simply try drinking or eating cold things more slowly.

Rain Forest Explorer's Journal

You're a biologist spending time in the Amazon. You've written about your findings, but now you must draw them.

Killer Parrots

Don't let the beautiful plumage of these birds fool you: they have razor sharp beaks, pointy claws, and dragon-like spiked tails.

The Lettered Butterfly

This colorful butterfly's markings resemble all the letters of the alphabet.

The Turtle Lizard

Has a lizard's tail, claws, and tongue, but strangely, has a turtle's shell.

The Bearded Monkey
Looks like a regular monkey, except for its exceptionally bushy beard.

What else did you find?

Haunted Highways and Ghostly Getaways

The highways and byways, and even the train tracks of North America are home to many ghostly apparitions—if you believe in that sort of thing. The hotels and motels have their fair share, too. Try reading these spooky travel tales out loud so that all your travel partners can hear them. These stories have an even eerier effect if you read them at night on a lonely highway, using only a small flashlight to illuminate the page. Or try reading them in the semi-darkness of your hotel room or tent. Use your most dramatic, spooky storyteller voice and even your parents will get goose bumps. If you're easily spooked, you might not want to read on. And whatever you do, don't stop for hitchhikers!

The Phantom Hitchhiker

It was a dark and stormy night. A family was driving down a deserted road, tired and far from their destination. They were about to stop for the night, when they saw a girl—probably no older than 18 years old—on the side of the road in a formal gown, with no raincoat or umbrella. She held out her thumb as she saw their van approach.

The mother looked at the father, who was driving. "Honey, we should pick her up. She must be freezing out there."

"You know we have a 'no hitchhiker' rule," he replied. "Don't want to set a bad example for the kids." He glanced over his shoulder at the tired children in the back.

"Something must have happened to her. Look at the way she's dressed," the mother said. "What if she were one of our kids? We would want a nice family to help her."

"Oh, all right," said the father pulling over. "Just this once..."

The girl got in the van, soaking wet, and moved to the unoccupied seat in the middle. "Thank you so much for stopping!" she said. "I was coming home from the school dance, and my car rolled all the way over into the ditch. Would you mind taking me home? It's just about three miles up the road."

The father followed her directions toward a home in a nice neighborhood. Along the way, she laughed and joked with the kids. Everyone was very happy that they had stopped to help her. But when they opened the door to let her out, she had vanished. The mother was concerned. She went to the front door of the house and rang the bell.

"I'm sorry to disturb you," she said to the woman who answered the door. "We gave your daughter a ride back here, and we didn't get to say goodbye."

The woman in the house looked at the mother with shock. "My daughter died this very night, three years ago, while coming home from a school dance. Her car crashed on the main road about three miles back."

The Ghostly Bellman

A family arrived at the beautiful castle-like hotel late on a cold winter's night. They had been driving all day through the Canadian Rockies and were happy to have such a marvelous place to stay. They checked into their room and a nice elderly bellman helped them with their bags. The three children went out to explore the hotel. They ran down the hallways and played hide and seek while their parents unpacked their bags. As the kids played, they kept running into the bellman in the hallway. He was very friendly and even showed them some good hiding places. He told them his name was Sam.

When their parents came looking for them, the children told them about the hiding places the bellman had shown them. When they were eating dinner at the hotel restaurant, the children's father mentioned the bellman to the waitress. "You kids met Sam?" she asked. "He was the head bellman here for many years. But he died 30 years before you were even born."

The Ghosts of the "Queen Mary"

Before it docked permanently in Long Beach, California, the "Queen Mary" was one of the most famous luxurious cruise ships in the world. Movie stars, heads of state, and wealthy patrons from all over the world walked its decks and enjoyed its many forms of entertainment: the ballrooms, movie theater, and swimming pool. In fact, some guests are said to have enjoyed it so much that they have chosen to stay there permanently.

Now a hotel, the "Queen Mary" is said to be haunted by a number of ghosts. Water is heard splashing in an empty swimming pool, and wet footprints are seen leading from the deck to the changing rooms. Women in vintage bathing suits have been spotted walking around the deck.

The St. Louis Ghost Train

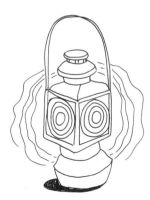

The year was 1898. A steam train chugged down a lonely stretch of tracks in Northern Saskatchewan, making its way through the foggy darkness. The conductor was having a hard time seeing what was ahead on the tracks. He grabbed his lantern and went to the door, sticking his head out to get a better look. Just at that moment, the train entered a tunnel. SNAP! The conductor's head fell off and rolled somewhere into the darkness.

The train stopped running long ago, and the tracks have even been removed, but on the old rail bed, the ghost train of St. Louis still rolls on. Countless people have seen its headlight moving steadily toward a destination it will never reach. Its yellow-white headlight is followed by a smaller, reddish glow—the light of the conductor's lantern as he searches for his head.

Write Your Own Ghost Story

Use the checklist below to create your own nightmare-inducing tale. Then tell it to your fellow travelers (unless, of course, you don't want to share your hotel room with someone who's tossing and turning).

☐ Describe the weather. It should probably be threatening, but you don't have to stick to "dark and stormy." Add some fog if you wish.

☐ Provide information that will haunt each sense. Include unexplained sights such as footprints in weird places, graphic descriptions of tingly feelings like spider legs crawling up an arm, and creepiness of every kind. Since ghost stories tend to be about dark places, sounds are especially important. Howling, thumping, tapping, groaning, and dripping—there are lots of possibilities.

☐ Increase the sense of dread as the story progresses. Give little hints in the beginning that the reader should be worried and add creepy details as you go. But make the ghostly (or gory or gross) conclusion a surprise. Reveal it suddenly at the end. (Here's where the sounds "Boo!" and "Gotcha!" come in handy.)

☐ Make sure the ghost has a past and a reason for haunting.

☐ Your evil spirits shouldn't be too obvious. They can be invisible, of course. Or they can just be tricky, and try to act like they're normal or nice. Keep it interesting by letting your listeners believe the characters have a chance of escaping and surviving.

☐ Strangers in period clothing could make an appearance. (Old clothes rustle and smell funny, after all.)

☐ Go ahead, tell them this story actually happened. Good fiction is the one good excuse for lying.

☐ These things help set the scene:
  • deserted highway
  • ramshackle cabin
  • hitchhiker
  • graveyard
  • spiders
  • axes or chainsaws
  • things that don't work, such as doors, squeaky hinges, and lights that go out
  • vermin

☐ Here are some classic ghost story words & phrases
  • hair-raising   • shiver
  • specter   • spine chilling
  • bone rattling   • blood curdling
  • piercing scream   • spleen bursting (Ok, so we believe in coining new classics.)

☐ Just put it all together and get your ominous voice going.

Bats

Go batty—fill up this cave.

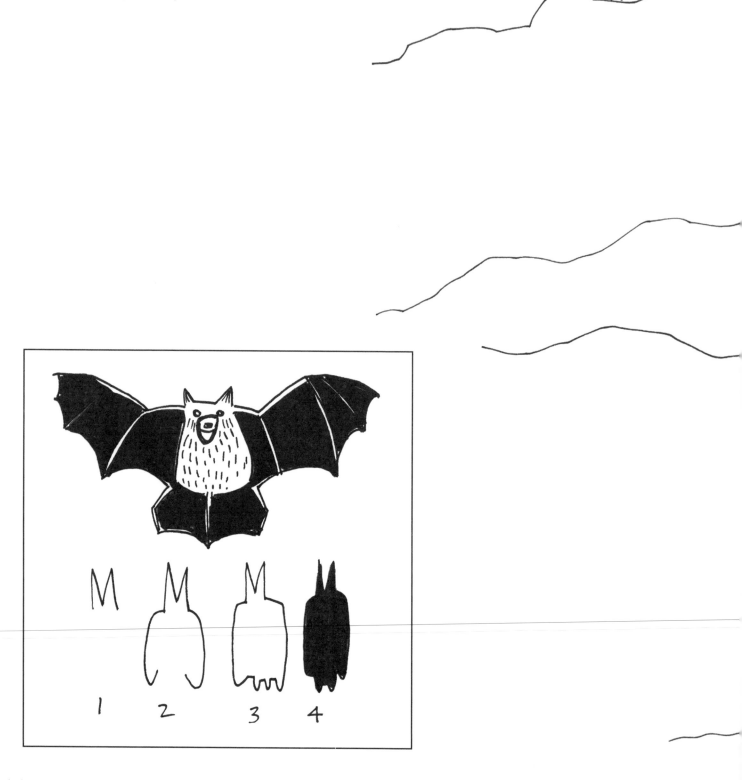

Chomp

Are you hungry for a game challenge? Take a bite out of Chomp. The game is played on an imaginary chocolate bar divided into different blocks. But beware: the top left block of the chocolate bar is poisoned! Whoever eats it, loses.

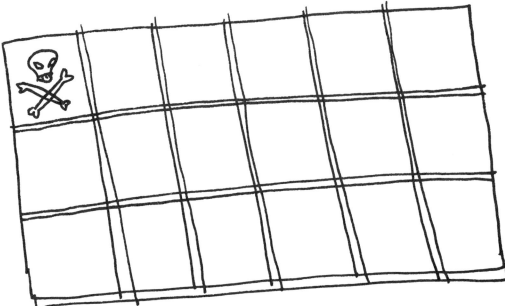

- Start with this 3 x 6 block "chocolate bar." You can make bigger ones later if you like. Just use the blank pages at the back of the book.

- Flip a coin to see who goes first.

- The first player chooses a block to "eat." When you eat a block, remove it, as well as any blocks below it and to its right. To do this, draw an X through the blocks.

- The next player chooses another block, again removing the blocks below and to the right of it.

- Play continues with players choosing and removing blocks.

- The top left block is "poisoned" and the player who has to eat it loses.

Nim

Like Chomp, Nim also involves removing objects from a group, but the rules are a little different. You can use any objects, and any number of objects to start with. For this example, the french fries are arranged in rows.

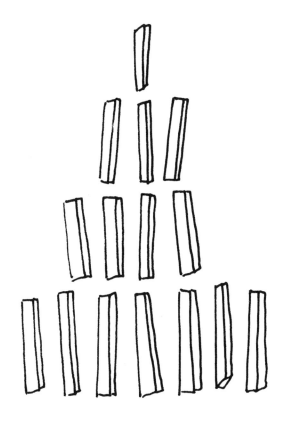

- Flip a coin to see who goes first.

- To play, the first player removes any number of french fries from a row. At least one must be taken, and all the fries removed must be from a single row.

- Play continues on the row the first player chose until all of the french fries have been removed. Then it's on to the next row.

- If you remove the last french fry, you win.

- Try the game using chips, coins, crayons, or anything you have on hand. Use any number of objects and create any number of rows. You can also create different rules. For example, say that a player must take away one, two, or three objects at a time.

- After you've played the game several times, you'll start to figure out a strategy that will help you win.

Whose Shoes, the Sequel

 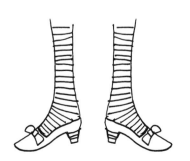 

My Guide to

_____
(insert name of destination)

Trips around the world, accommodations in fantastic resorts—such are the concerns of a travel writer, sent to review exotic destinations. If this sounds like the life for you, there's no time like the present to get started. Explore your destination through the eyes of a guidebook writer. Try to write down or remember details, such as how much stuff costs or how long you had to wait in line. When you get home, you can even share your review with other travelers by submitting it to a travel website.

Example:

Accommodation: The Fleabag Motel, Nowheresville, USA

Number of Stars: ★

Review: Hot water would have been nice. They didn't serve any food, but we could smell the fried chicken coming from the fast-food restaurant next door. The cable didn't work, but we were entertained by the sounds of people in the next room. We left with more than memories—we had flea bites on our ankles.

Recommendation: Sleep in your car instead!

Activity/Attraction: _____

Number of Stars: _____

Review: _____

_____

_____

_____

_____

Recommendation: _____

Restaurant: _____

Number of Stars: _____

Review: _____

_____

_____

_____

_____

Recommendation: _____

Accommodation: _____

Number of Stars: _____

Review: _____

_____

_____

_____

_____

Recommendation: _____

Activity/Attraction: _____

Number of Stars: _____

Review: _____

_____

_____

_____

_____

Recommendation: _____

Restaurant: _____

Number of Stars: _____

Review: _____

_____

_____

_____

_____

Recommendation: _____

Accommodation: _____

Number of Stars: _____

Review: _____

_____

_____

_____

_____

Recommendation: _____

Activity/Attraction: _____

Number of Stars: _____

Review: _____

_____

_____

_____

_____

Recommendation: _____

Restaurant: _____

Number of Stars: _____

Review: _____

_____

_____

_____

_____

Recommendation: _____

Accommodation: _____

Number of Stars: _____

Review: _____

_____

_____

_____

_____

Recommendation: _____

Road Signs

Devise your own.

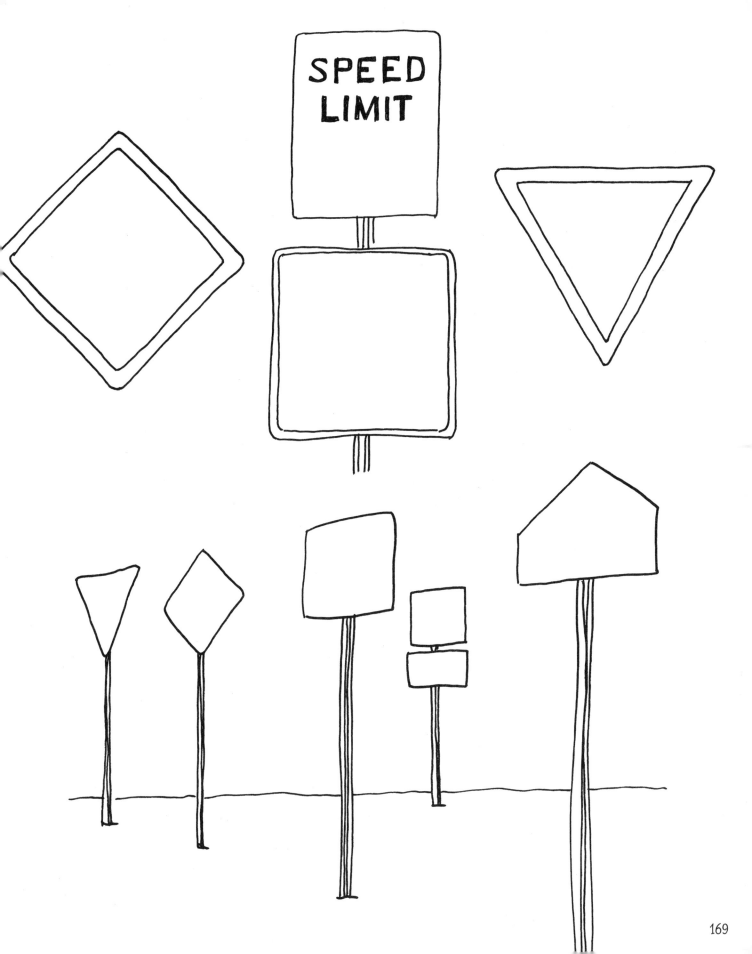

SPEED
LIMIT

Brain Jumpstart

Long trips can be tough on your brain. After a few hours, it can start to feel like its battery is running out of juice. Working through these puzzling problems will get your brain running at peak performance again. (Answers are on page 249.)

Crossing the River

A long time ago, in a city far away, a small group of people gathered by the side of a river and wondered how they would cross it. The group consisted of a mother, father, two sons, two daughters, a prison guard, and a thief. There was raft that could take people across the river, but there were many rules about who could board the raft:

• The raft could carry a maximum of two people at a time.

• The father could not stay with the daughters without their mother present.

• The mother could not stay with the sons without their father present.

• The thief could not stay with any family member if the prison guard wasn't there.

• Only the father, the mother, and the prison guard knew how to operate the raft. How did they all get across the river?

Use the space below to work out your answers...

The Night Watchman

Joe worked as a night watchman at a small factory. He had a dream that his boss had gotten on a plane that crashed. The next morning before the watchman went home, he rushed to his boss and told him not to take the flight he had planned for the day. He listened to Joe, and sure enough, the plane that the boss had planned to take crashed. He thanked Joe for saving his life. Then the boss fired him. Why?

How Many Fs?

You don't want to get any Fs at school, but for this puzzle, you're looking for as many as you can find.
Read the sentence and count the Fs as you read.

Finished files are the result of years of scientific study combined with the experience of years.

Think you know how many there are? Turn to page 249 to see if you got them all.

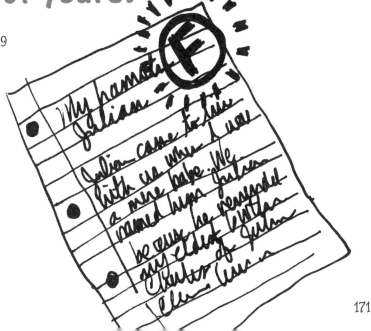

Face-off

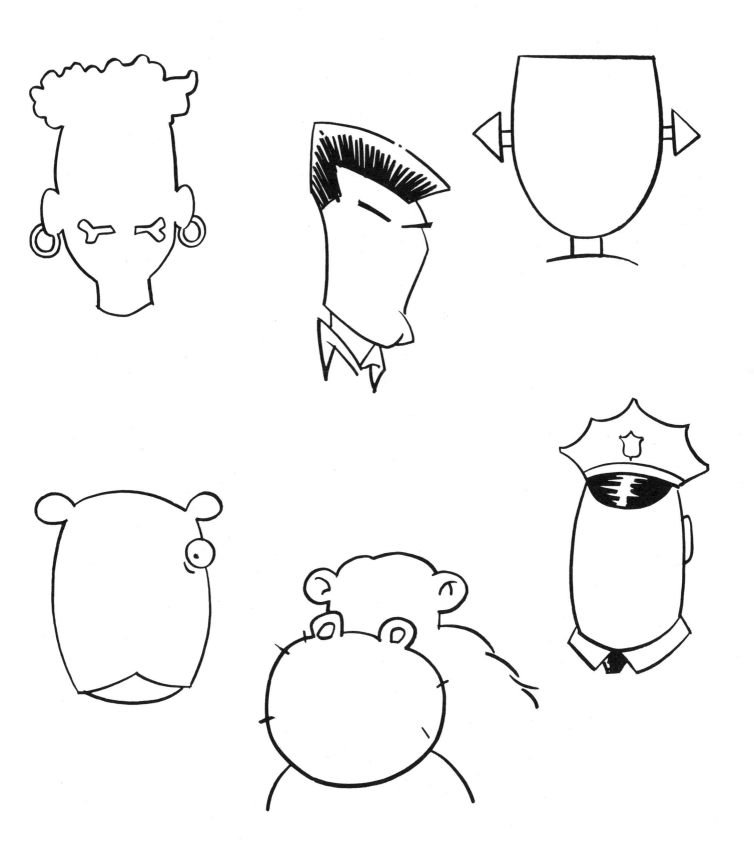

Hashi

Example 1

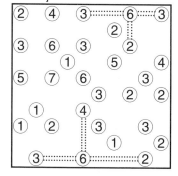

Example 2

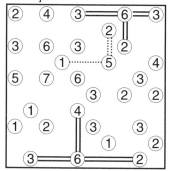

Example 3

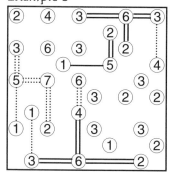

Example 4

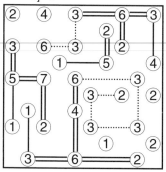

Hashi is short for "Hashiwokakero," which means "let's build bridges" in Japanese. And with these puzzles, that's just what you'll be doing. Each of the numbered "islands" in the puzzles need to be linked together by bridges. The number in each island dictates how many bridges it needs. But there are three rules you have to follow:

• The bridges can only be vertical or horizontal. No diagonal lines or wiggly lines allowed.

• Bridges can't cross other bridges.

• You can't have more than two bridges along any one route.

When you're done, every island should be connected to every other one. And there's only one correct solution for each puzzle. Answers on pages 249-250.

Here are some tips.

• Mark an "x" on completed islands

• Don't guess. Only make moves based on your deductions.

Starting off:

• Look for a 6-clue island in a side row. A side island can only have three neighbors, so each neighbor of a 6-clue island must have two bridges (Example 1). Since corners can only have two neighbors, a 4-clue island in the corner will also have two bridges for each neighbor (not shown).

• Check to see if any of your 1- or 2-clue islands have only one neighbor. Bridges must connect to that one neighbor (Example 2).

• Scan the puzzle to see how many bridges you can connect now. Look for islands that only need one more bridge and only have one more neighbor. Look for islands in which possible neighbors have been cut off by other bridges (Example 3).

• At this point, even if you can't figure out where all the bridges for a certain island go, you can make some logical decisions. For example, if there are any 3-clue islands with only two neighbors, you know each island gets at least one bridge (Example 4). Can you finish the puzzle now?

Puzzle 1

Puzzle 2

Puzzle 3

Puzzle 4

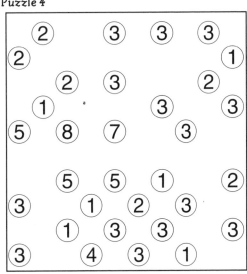

Puzzle 5

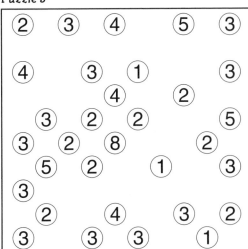

Puzzle 6

175

Puzzle 7

(2) (6) (3)   (2) (1)
(2) (3) (4) (4)   (4)
(3) (3) (6) (4) (3)
    (3) (1) (4)
  (1)   (2) (6)
(3)   (3)   (4)
  (2) (5) (3)
(2)   (2) (1) (2)

Puzzle 8

(1)   (4)   (2)
(1) (3)   (2)   (3)
(2) (8) (4)   (3) (3)
  (2) (4) (2)
(2) (7) (2) (1)   (3)
  (2) (4) (2)
(1)
  (2) (1) (4) (3)

Puzzle 9

(2) (3)   (3) (2)
(1)   (2)
(4) (8) (2)   (3)
  (2) (6) (3)
(3) (5) (3) (1) (4)
(3) (3) (5) (2)
(3) (1) (2)   (3)
(3) (2) (5) (3)
(2)   (1)
(2) (4) (3) (2)

Puzzle 10

(1) (3) (6)   (3)
(3) (3) (3) (1)
  (2)
(1) (4)   (4) (3)
(4) (3) (4) (2)
(3) (2) (3) (2)
(1) (2) (2)
(3) (7) (4) (3)
  (1)
(2) (4) (3) (3) (3)

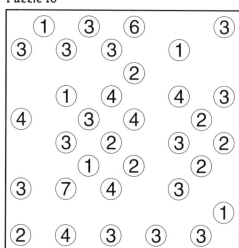

Puzzle 11

(2) (3) (4) (2)
(2) (4) (2) (3)
  (3) (2)
(4) (6) (6) (3) (3)
(1) (2)
(4)   (4) (3)
(2) (4)
(4) (2) (2) (2) (6)
(1) (3) (2) (1)
(2) (3) (3) (1) (3)

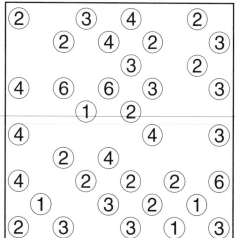

Puzzle 12

(2) (1) (3) (2)
  (1) (2)
(6) (4)   (2)
(2) (2) (2) (4)
(3) (3)
(4) (4)
(3) (3) (5) (3)
(2) (4) (3) (2) (2)
(2) (1) (2)
(2) (4) (4) (2) (3)

176

Puzzle 13

(2) (6) (4)　(5) (3)
　　(1)　(2) (2)
(1)　　　(2) (2)
　(2) (2) (4) (3)
(3)　(4) (2) (1)
　(1)　(2)　(4)
(3)　(4)　(3) (2)
　(2)　(3) (4) (3)
(2)　　　(1)
　(2) (3) (2) (3) (3)

Puzzle 14

(2) (4)　(4)　(2)
　　　(1)　(2)
(3) (8) (2)
　　(1) (3) (3) (4)
(4) (7) (4) (2) (1)
(3) (3)　(2) (6) (3)
　　(2) (1)
(1)
　(3)　(2) (5) (2)

Puzzle 15

(3) (2) (4) (2)　(3)
　(2) (1)
(3) (1) (4)　(2) (3)
　　　　(1)
　(3)　(4)　(2)
(3) (2)　　(3)
　(2)　(6) (2)
(3) (3)　(2) (8) (4)
　　(3) (1)
(1) (3)　(3) (5) (2)

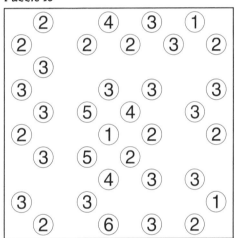

Puzzle 16

　(2)　(4) (3) (1)
(2)　(2) (2) (3) (2)
　(3)
(3)　(3) (3)　(3)
　(3) (5) (4)　(3)
(2)　(1) (2)　(2)
　(3) (5) (2)
　　(4) (3) (3)
(3)　(3)　　(1)
　(2)　(6) (3) (2)

Puzzle 17

(2) (6) (3) (3)　(2)
(3) (5) (5) (6) (2)
(3)　(2)　(2) (4)
　(3)　(3) (2)
(4)　(1) (4) (3) (4)
　(3) (1) (2) (2)
(2)　(2) (4) (1) (2)
　(3) (3) (4) (3)

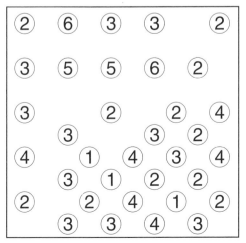

Puzzle 18

(2)　(4) (3) (2)
　　　　(2) (3)
(2) (1) (6) (3) (2)
　(2) (1)
(4) (3) (8)　(3) (3)
　(2)　(4) (3) (3)
(3) (2)　(3) (2) (2)
(1)　　(2) (3)
(2) (2)　(2) (3) (3)

Swap Out

Draw with your non-dominant hand. For example, if you're right handed, draw with your left hand. Try signing your name with your non-dominant hand. Keep trying until you get good at it. Now, hold the pencil any way except the way you would normally. Grip it by your thumb and pinkie, for example.

Haiku for You

Haiku is a type of poetry first perfected in Japan hundreds of years ago. Haiku have three lines with five, seven, and five syllables, respectively. Have a go at the unfinished haiku below. Each dot in the blanks below represent a syllable. When you're done, create some that are completely your own.

Cupcakes and ice cream

Candy, soda, frosted flakes

• •
_____ cavities

Monday morning knock

•   •   •   •
_____ time for school

Covers over head

Donkey stomps a beat

Hen hums cow croons sow shimmies

Barnyard _____
•   •   •

Boo hoo boo hoo hoo

Ha ha ha hee hee haw haw

•   •   •   •   •
_____

What I said was _____
•

What I meant was _____
•   •   •

Mouth, brain, not attached

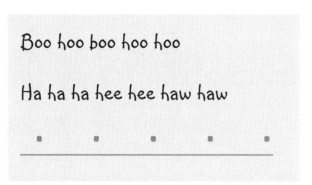

Didn't make my bed

•   •   •   •   •   •   •
_____

•   •   •
_____ big deal

Sit around _____ fire

Roasting _____ on sticks

Tell _____ stories

_____ good book

_____ travel _____

Never leave your chair

Summer night _____

_____ embers gleam

_____ fireflies

_____ underwear

_____ outerwear

_____ everywhere

Test in _____ class

Study hard _____

Hope I don't _____ it

_____ animal

Feet like _____, trunk like _____

Tromps through _____

TV _____

So much _____ left undone

_____ instead

Lunchroom _____

Mashed potatoes _____

_____ food fight

For Word Game Lovers!

Would you rather do a crossword puzzle than ride your bike? Do word jumbles make you smile? If so, look no further—these pages are for you!

Word Golf

Lewis Carroll, the author of **Alice's Adventures in Wonderland**, invented this game. The goal is to turn one word into another by substituting single letters and using the fewest steps possible.

Let's say you wanted to turn CAT into DOG.

Here's an example:

CAT

COT

DOT

DOG

You've done it in three steps, so you get three points.

Here are the rules:

- Choose a starting word and an ending word. The starting and ending words must be the same length. For example, you could turn "Good" into "Book," but not into "Bad."

- While beginning, it's best to try simple words with fewer letters.

- Each player gets the same words, but you shouldn't peek at others' work.

- A new English word must be formed with every step. Only one letter can be substituted per step.

- When a player is done, he reveals his word to the other player. Points are counted based on the number of words it took to transform the word.

- The player with the lowest score at the end of the game wins.

Target

How many words can you make from the letters in the grids? Your words can be any length, but you can't use any letters more than once unless they're repeated in the grid. We have four separate games for you below. For an added challenge, only count four-letter words. How many words can you come up with always using the middle letter?

R	O	D
E	P	E
E	V	L

R	C	R
Y	T	F
E	O	E

R	I	G
E	T	A
C	R	I

E	L	P
O	B	I
R	O	T

Here's your target:

15 words = great

10 words = very good

8 words = good

5 words = keep trying!

Ghost

Despite its name, this game isn't spooky—it's just a word game. The only thing you need to play is two to four players, paper, something to write with, and a good vocabulary.

How to Play:

- The object of the game is to keep adding letters to a possible word without actually forming one. Make sense? It will in a moment.

- Choose who goes first. Play will continue in a clockwise direction.

- With a possible word in mind, the first player writes a single letter from that word on a piece of paper. The next player thinks about what word could be made from that letter and adds another letter, either before or after the first. Play continues this way, with players trying to keep the word growing for as long as possible. The round is over when a player has no other choice but to complete the word. Don't forget about suffixes and prefixes!

Here's an Example:

E
ET
ETA
ETAT
ETATI
ETATIO
GETATIO
EGETATIO
VEGETATIO
VEGETATION

- Remember that prefixes and suffixes will help your game. If it looks like you might lose on the word IMAGINE, set it up so that your opponent is forced to add the last letter to REIMAGINE.

- Of course there's always the plural strategy as well. REIMAGINES is also a valid word, so you could have added an S to IMAGINE instead of an R.

Ghosting

What if you have your doubts that the word fragment your opponent just added a letter to is actually part of a real word? Call for a challenge (this is called "ghosting" someone). If the person you've challenged can't tell you what the word is, you win the round. But be warned: if she does have a real word in mind, you lose.

Bluffing

It's possible to bluff in Ghost. For example, you can pretend to add a suffix to a word, even if that word doesn't exist. If no one challenges you, you can continue with the nonexistent word.

Scoring

You don't have to keep score, but if you do, it's done the same way as in HORSE, the basketball game. The player who loses the first round gets a G, the next an H, and so on. The player who accumulates all the letters to GHOST first loses, and the game is over.

It Came From Outer Space

This object just crashed to Earth in a meteor shower. Scientists believe it came from the planet Beljar in a distant galaxy.

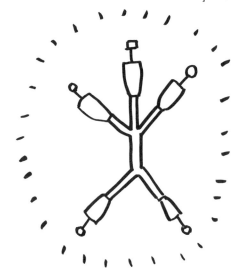

What is it?

What do the inhabitants of Beljar do with it?

If humans can touch it, what does it feel like?

What use might humans have for it?

What should humans do if the Beljarians want it back?

Beljarians: "Give us our thing back...."

raw a picture of the alien item as it's used in its natural environment.

185

Finger Baseball

Finger baseball has all (or at least some) of the excitement and drama of regular baseball, but it's played by really tiny players—your fingers. They'll do all the pitching, hitting, running, and scoring. Just like regular baseball, the goal of finger baseball is to have the most runs at the end of nine innings. (If the game ends in a tie, you can go into extra innings, too). You may never make the major leagues in real baseball, but in finger baseball, it's easy to be a champ.

How to Play

- One player is the pitcher and the other is the batter.

- The pitcher starts the game by saying, "One, two, three, shoot!"

- Both players then "shoot" their fingers at the same time, choosing to show one, two, three, or four fingers (sort of the way you would show your hand in Rock, Paper, Scissors).

- If the numbers the players are showing don't match (for example, if the pitcher shows three fingers and the batter shows two), the batter is out.

- If the numbers do match, the batter gets a hit. The number of fingers shown determines the base the batter reaches. If it's one finger, she gets to first. If it's two, she gets to second, and so on. If batter and pitcher both show four, the batter gets a home run.

- Each batter gets three outs per inning, and then the other player becomes the batter. After the end of nine innings, the player with the highest score wins.

- Now here's where play gets a little trickier. Let's say you're the batter. You have a base runner on second base (because you and the pitcher both held out two fingers). On your next at bat, you get a single (both held out one finger). Your runner at second moves to third. At your third at bat, you get a double (base runner makes it to second). That advances the runner on third to home and the runner on first moves two bases to third. You score one run with runners on second and third.

Those are the basic rules. If you want to make the game more challenging, there are some other rules to throw into the mix on the following page.

Hit & Run

In real baseball, if a runner is on second and a single is hit, there's a chance the runner might be able to run all the way home. In finger baseball, you can try the same thing. After hitting a single, the batter can call "hit and run" to see if his runner on second will score. Both players shoot again, this time using only three fingers. If there's a match, the runner on second can score. If not, he is out at home.

Sacrifice Fly

After a batter makes an out and if there are less than two outs, she can try for a sacrifice fly to advance a runner on third to home. The batter calls for a "sacrifice fly." The players shoot again, using only three fingers. If there's a match, the runner on third will score. If not, the runner on third is out.

Double Plays

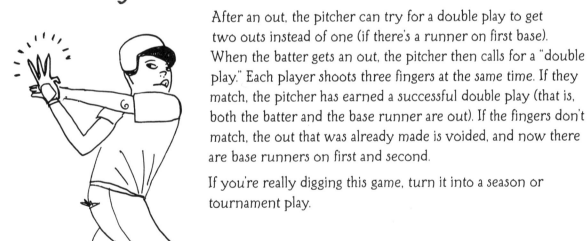

After an out, the pitcher can try for a double play to get two outs instead of one (if there's a runner on first base). When the batter gets an out, the pitcher then calls for a "double play." Each player shoots three fingers at the same time. If they match, the pitcher has earned a successful double play (that is, both the batter and the base runner are out). If the fingers don't match, the out that was already made is voided, and now there are base runners on first and second.

If you're really digging this game, turn it into a season or tournament play.

Best in Show

Add colors, clothes, and dogs, and then decide which one gets "best in show."

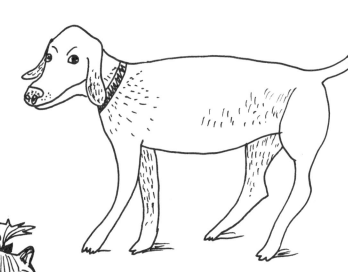

What's the Story?

Reading in the car might give you a headache, but making up your own stories won't! Try one of these storytelling games and find out how creative your fellow travelers really are.

Fortunately, Unfortunately

This game can be played with any number of players, but it's better if you have at least three.

How to Play

* Decide who goes first. The first person begins with a sentence. It could be absolutely anything—for example: "One day a princess kissed a frog."

* The next person tells of something unfortunate that happens: "Unfortunately, the frog was covered with flesh-eating bacteria, which the princess quickly contracted."

* The third person changes the story once more by adding a fortunate event: "Fortunately, the frog that she kissed turned into a Doctor of Infectious Diseases who was able to quickly administer a round of antibiotics."

* The story goes on like this until it feels like it has reached its logical conclusion.

Consequences

Even though everyone takes part in this game, no one knows what the story is until the end. This game is more fun if three or more people play.

How to Play

- *Use a blank piece of paper. Leaving space in between each, write these categories down the left side of the page:*

    Man's name

    Woman's name

    Place name

    A comment

    Another comment

    An outcome

- The first player writes down a man's name, folds the paper so that his entry can't be seen, and passes the page to the next person.

- The next player writes a woman's name, folds the page and then passes it on to the next person who writes a place name. And so on until the last entry has been made.

- The last player connects the entries with the following words:

    Man's name

    MET

    Woman's name

    AT

    Place name

    AND HE SAID

    A comment

    AND SHE SAID

    Another comment

    AND SO

    An outcome.

- *Then she reads the story aloud.*

- A sample story might read: Paul met Donna at the skate park, and he said, "What nice teeth you have," and she said, "There's no place like home," and so the building exploded.

- *Once you have the idea down, you can play differently by substituting other people or animals for the man or woman. Change the comments to actions. Or you could have the last player decide how to construct the story based on what everyone has written.*

Outer Space Explorer's Journal

You're the first human to explore Mars. Here's a record of your findings.
Now fill in the pictures.

Martian Trees
They have many more branches than Earth trees; and their leaves have very unusual shapes.

Martian Flowers
Like nothing we've ever seen on Earth. I really can't describe them. You've just got to see them!

Martian Insects
Hundreds of legs; bright colors; big eyes; very sharp, spear-like antennae.

Martian Birds
They're a bit like flamingos, but they've got two heads and very, very long beaks.

What *else* did you find?

Super You!

Faster than a speeding bullet, able to leap tall buildings in a single bound—these abilities could come in handy some time, like on your school's Field Day. Imagine you really are a superhero. What would your name be? What would your outfit look like? Do you have a cape? A mask? What would your superpowers be?

Draw yourself as a superhero.

Name: _____

Powers: _____

Do you have a secret identity, such as Peter Parker (Spider-Man) or Clark Kent (Superman)? How does your alter ego keep his/her superpowers a secret? _____

_____

_____

Draw your sidekick.

Draw your nemesis.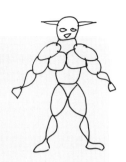

Name: _____

What does he/she help you do? _____

_____

_____

_____

_____

Name: _____

What powers does he/she have and how are they used for evil? _____

_____

_____

_____

Framed!

You know what to do.

The Chinese Zodiac

Are you a rat or a monkey? That means, are you charming or a genius? The Chinese Zodiac measures time in a 12-year cycle based on the moon. An animal represents each of those years. People are supposed to have qualities like the animal for the year they were born. So, people born in the Year of the Monkey are said to be as smart as monkeys.

Find your birth year and animal below. This is a simple version of the Chinese Zodiac. A serious reading involves the day and hour of your birth and much more. But deciding if these descriptions fit your personality or the personalities of people you know can still get you thinking.

Rat
1912, 1924, 1936, 1948, 1960, 1972, 1984, 1996, 2008
People are naturally attracted to you and you are likely to succeed. But don't focus on what you want so much that you forget your friends. It's natural for you to be friends with Dragons and Monkeys. It's more of a challenge to get along with Horses.

Ox
1913, 1925, 1937, 1949, 1961, 1973, 1985, 1997, 2009
You're patient, hardworking, and dependable. Being steady is good, as long as you learn not to get mad when people have other ideas or things change. Snakes and Roosters are your closest friends. You may be tempted to argue with Sheep.

Tiger
1914, 1926, 1938, 1950, 1962, 1974, 1986, 1998, 2010
You're brave, smart, and other people like your ideas. But don't make decisions recklessly because you're excited. It's easy for you to get along with Horses and Dogs, but not Monkeys.

Rabbit
1915, 1927, 1939, 1951, 1963, 1975, 1987, 1999, 2011
People born in the Year of the Rabbit are polite with great talent and taste. Just don't take those qualities too far and act snobby or disinterested. Sheep or Boars are most like you. Your opposite is the Rooster.

Dragon
1916, 1928, 1940, 1952, 1964, 1976, 1988, 2000, 2012
You're full of energy. You're sure of yourself. And why not? You're lucky, too. But you can behave very strangely and make bad decisions. Monkeys and Rats make you happy, but you might not choose to spend time with Dogs.

Snake

1917, 1929, 1941, 1953, 1965, 1977, 1989, 2001, 2013

You're quiet and think deeply. But sometimes you want to take care of everything by yourself so much that you *seem* selfish or unfriendly. You're more likely to be best friends with a Rooster or Ox than any other animal—especially the Boar.

Horse

1918, 1930, 1942, 1954, 1966, 1978, 1990, 2002, 2014

People born in the Year of the Horse are quick, funny, and talkative. But you don't always listen to what others say and can be impatient. Get to know Tigers and Dogs, but don't be surprised if you don't spend time with many Rats.

Sheep

1919, 1931, 1943, 1955, 1967, 1979, 1991, 2003, 2015

If you were born in the Year of the Sheep, you're artistic and understanding. As much as you like other people, you can be awkward and you worry a lot. Your friends will probably be Boars and Rabbits—not Oxen.

Monkey

1920, 1932, 1944, 1956, 1968, 1980, 1992, 2004, 2016

You're clever and come up with unique ways to solve problems. Don't get frustrated with projects or people who don't move as fast as you. Don't enjoy Tigers' company? Dragons and Rats are a better fit.

Rooster

1921, 1933, 1945, 1957, 1969, 1981, 1993, 2005, 2017

People born in the Year of the Rooster are confident, responsible, and do a good job. Even if you are usually right, don't be a pushy perfectionist. Snakes and Oxen are the most like you. You're least likely to agree with Rabbits.

Dog

1922, 1934, 1946, 1958, 1970, 1982, 1994, 2006, 2018

You stand by friends and beliefs—to the point of being stubborn. You're attractive to others, but can *seem* like you're not interested in them. Horses or Tigers are your friends. But dogs are rarely friends with Dragons.

Pig

1923, 1935, 1947, 1959, 1971, 1983, 1995, 2007, 2019

You're strong, hardworking, honest, and a good friend. But you can be fooled easily and care too much about possessions. Most Pigs have more fun with Rabbits and Sheep than with other Pigs.

Tag-Team Drawing

Recruit everyone who's not driving to help create a drawing. Start off by drawing a line, squiggle, or simple shape. (Don't tell anyone what you have in mind for the picture.) Pass the picture along to the next person and have them add to it. Keep passing it and adding stuff until the paper is covered or you conclude that you have a masterwork.

The Spooky Survival Quiz

Do you know what to do when zombies attack? Would you be caught unprepared if a vampire showed up at your door?

Take this quiz. Then check your answers on page 251.

1. A werewolf is approaching. You should:

    A. Shoot him with a silver bullet.
    B. Make the sign of the cross.
    C. Shine a light in his eyes.
    D. Show him his face in a mirror.

2. If you want to vampire-proof your house, you should:

    A. Mark above the door with blood.
    B. Make sure it's well lit.
    C. Hang garlic above the door.
    D. Paint a cross on the door.

3. A horde of zombies is coming down the street. You can stop the zombies by:

    A. Throwing rocks in their path.
    B. Bathing frequently—because they can't see, they can only find you through their sense of smell.
    C. Running as fast as you can—zombies are slow movers.
    D. Nothing can stop a zombie (you're out of luck).

4. Your house is haunted. How can you rid it of annoying ghosts?

    A. Hire an exterminator.
    B. You can't—just move.
    C. Have a discussion with the ghost and politely ask him to leave.
    D. Get a cat—ghosts hate cats.

5. All of the following can be used to ward off trolls except:

    A. Church bells
    B. Anything made of steel
    C. A wreath of daisies
    D. A cross

6. Some witches are nice. But others you'd rather steer clear of. Which of these is NOT a way to keep them away?

A. Putting a rosemary plant on your doorstep.
B. Hanging a hagstone (a stone with a hole in it) on your bedpost.
C. Wearing a protective amulet.
D. Hanging a silver bell above the door.

7. There you are, wrapped in a cocoon, hanging upside down in the web of a giant spider. How do you get out?

A. Use something sharp in your pocket to cut the strands around you.
B. When the spider unravels the cocoon to eat you, poke it hard in as many of its eyes as you can.
C. Sorry, there's really no way out.
D. Spiders are sensitive to sound—try an ear-splitting scream.

8. If you find yourself in a battle with a dragon, what's the best way to get out alive?

A. Run.
B. Bribe it with gold.
C. Find a missing scale so you can plunge your sword into its hide.
D. Sprinkle sleeping powder under its nose.

Draw These

Wanderlist!

At this very moment, you may be on your way to Aunt Zelda's house in Possum City. But don't worry. If this trip isn't exactly your idea of a great vacation, you've got plenty of time left to explore the world and visit your dream destinations. Think about the places you most want to see and list your top 10 choices. Making a list is the first step toward making it happen!

Top 10 Places I Want to See

1. _____
2. _____
3. _____
4. _____
5. _____

6. _____
7. _____
8. _____
9. _____
10. _____

Join the Club!

If you get started soon, you may someday be able to join the Traveler's Century Club, a group open to anyone who has visited 100 countries or more. There are 315 "countries" on the club's official list of places that count toward that total. Some of them are actually part of other countries, but since they are culturally different or geographically distant, the club recognizes them as separate. "Visiting" the country requires no more than a stop at an airport or port. Club member Charles Veley is said to be the world's most traveled man. He's been to 518 countries, territories, and islands—and he did it in just five years.

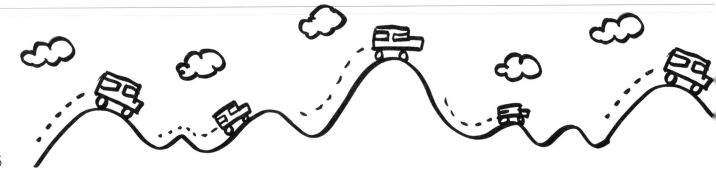

Visit If You Dare!

Most people would agree, it's good to stay away from war zones or places
with a reputation for lots of crime. Haunted places are often best avoided, too,
as are those with extreme temperatures. Some places appeal to a few people
but repel many. Bracken Caves, near San Antonio, Texas, are really cool if you love bats.
If you don't like bat poo, however, you might want to stay away. The millions of bats who make their
home there don't use toilets. Millions of bats, eating several times a day, year after year? You do the math—
it's a lot of poo. The rat temple in Deshnoke, India, is another place that's not for the squeamish. The fur is
always flying (or scurrying, actually) in this beautiful Hindu temple where more than 20,000 rats are fed,
protected, and worshipped as holy creatures. If skeletons scare you, don't go to the "bone chapel" in Kutna
Hora, outside of Prague, Czech Republic. It's decorated with more than 40,000 human bones and skulls.

10 Places I Really Don't Want to Go

1. _____
2. _____
3. _____
4. _____
5. _____

6. _____
7. _____
8. _____
9. _____
10. _____

The Lazy Kid's Travel Journal

Here's an easy way to record your travel experiences without having to do too much thinking. Just ask one of your travel companions to provide the parts of speech listed under each blank. Then read aloud your instant travel journal and see how closely it matches the trip you're taking.

Day _____
(number)

     Well, we're finally off on our trip to _____. The day started out _____.
(place name)   (adverb)

The weather was _____ and it made me feel _____ about the journey ahead. I
(adjective)   (adjective)

thought that I would feel _____, but was surprised that the _____ was
(adjective)   (noun)

_____.
(adjective)

     The whole time we were on our way, I kept _____-ing. I was starting to get really
(verb)

_____. I thought it was _____, but boy was I _____. _____
(adjective)   (adjective)   (adjective)   (name of person)

kept _____-ing the whole time. It was really _____.
(verb)   (adjective)

     When we'd been in the _____ a while, we saw this _____ that was pretty
(noun)   (noun)

_____. I don't think I've ever _____ anything like that before.
(adjective)   (verb—past tense)

     So far we've seen a lot of _____ that are really _____. I wish I'd had my
(plural noun)   (adjective)

_____ with me so I could _____.
(noun)   (verb)

     I know I'm going to have a lot of _____ on this trip, but the thing I'm really looking
(noun)

forward to is _____. That is going to be really _____. In the meantime, I'm just
(noun or verb)   (adjective)

going to _____ and hope that _____ doesn't _____. More later!
(verb)   (noun)   (verb)

Word supply

If you're really lazy, don't even bother to come up with your own adverbs, adjectives, nouns, and verbs. Just borrow some from this list.

Adjectives	Adverbs	Nouns	Verbs
annoying	accidentally	airplane	arrive
awful	badly	animals	break
awesome	easily	car	bring
beautiful	happily	bathroom	buy
big	nervously	beach	catch
bored	often	book	climb
brave	politely	brother	feel
clean	quickly	cloud	freeze
cold	suspiciously	dog	hate
creepy	slow	father	hear
crowded	suddenly	food	leave
cute	well	houses	lose
enormous	worse	mother	love
famous		mountains	ride
fancy		people	see
far		rain	smell
friendly		seat	snore
full		sister	switch
funny		tire	taste
gross		trees	touch
grumpy			try
hot			wander
hungry			watch
incredible			write
long			
loud			
lucky			
near			
rainy			
rotten			
sleepy			
smelly			
stormy			
super			
thirsty			
tiny			

Sticky Situations

Stick figures may not have mouths, but that doesn't mean they can't have conversations.
What do you think these figures could be talking about?

Make your own stick-figure funnies in the empty panels.

Paper Soccer

Ball sports and confined spaces don't go well together. But if you absolutely can't wait until you get to your destination to play ball, try this game. In Paper Soccer, the object of the game is the same as in real soccer: to get your "ball" into the opponent's goal. This is done one "kick" at a time. You use your pencil to kick instead of your foot, but at least there are no penalties and there's no risk of getting kicked in the shins. Several playing fields are on the opposite page.

How To Play

- Your imaginary ball is the dot on the center line of the field. Play starts from this point.

- Flip a coin to see who goes first. Each player is then assigned a side of the field and a goal. Your aim is to get the ball into your opponent's goal.

- The first player can move the ball vertically, horizontally, or diagonally into any of the surrounding squares. In any one turn, the ball can move one space.

- A line is drawn on the field to show the movement of the ball.

- The next player "picks up" the ball from its last position and tries to move it back toward the opponent's goal.

- The trick is that no lines can be crossed. When play reaches the border of the field, the ball can be "bounced" back in any possible direction and the player gets another turn.

- Both players need to strategize their moves so that the ball stays in play.

- The winner is the first player to reach the opponent's goal.

- If a player gets to a point where she can't make any more valid moves, she automatically loses.

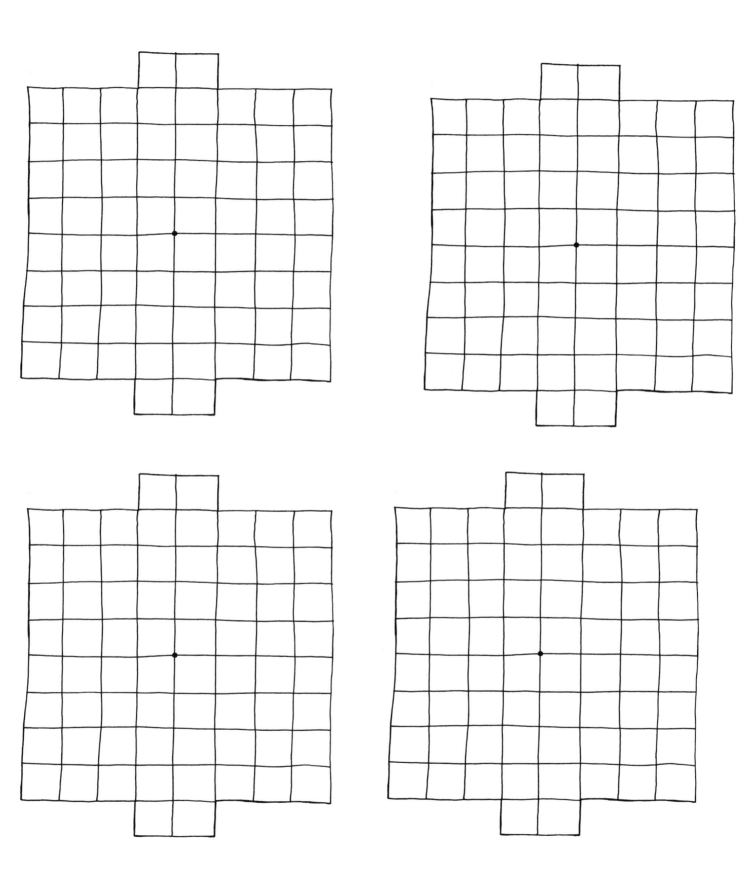

Secret Mission

Your mission, should you choose to accept it...

For this trip, each traveler will have a secret mission known only to him. It is the job of every other traveler to figure out what it is that her fellow travelers are up to. This game plays out over the course of time, so don't try to speed it up!

How to Proceed

* Ask someone not playing the game to tear out the missions on the opposite page. The nonplayer should then fold each mission in half and put them in a container.

* Each traveler chooses a mission, keeping it secret.

* No immediate action will be necessary upon receiving your mission. Rather, you will need to act upon it when the opportunity arises. You'll need to pay attention to opportunities to carry out your mission.

* Don't be too obvious—subtlety is your goal.

* Anyone can make a guess at a fellow traveler's mission at any time. If the person guesses incorrectly, the traveler only needs to shake his head.

* Once your mission has been guessed, you can still continue to guess the missions of others.

* The last person whose mission is revealed is the super spy!

Secret Missions

You will act overly surprised every time someone tells you something.

You will offer to help at every possible opportunity.

You will continually claim to see things out the window that aren't really there.

You will enthusiastically proclaim the deliciousness of everything you eat.

You will quietly hum a certain tune on and off throughout the day.

You will read aloud the words on signs that you pass whenever possible.

You will not finish most of your sentences, trailing off in a distracted way before you get to the end.

You will be the last one to exit the car, enter a building, and leave the table all day.

You will start using an expression—such as "Gee whiz" or "Awesome" or "I'll say"—that your travel partners have never heard you use before.

You will be continually nostalgic for home, wondering aloud what people are doing at home, what the weather is like there, etc.

You will make sound effects any time you do something such as shut a door, open a can, drop something, or any other time it seems possible.

Anytime someone asks you a question, you will get a far-away look in your eyes before giving your answer.

Napkin Art

There aren't too many car (or airplane seat) friendly crafts, but here's one that requires nothing but a paper napkin. Your parents probably have some on hand. If not, you can pick some up at your next food stop.

Perfect Picnic Pocket

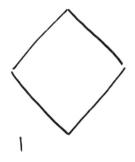 1

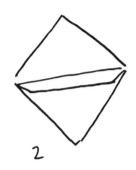 2

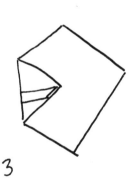 3

 4

 5

Use a square napkin—the kind that is folded into four layers—for this project. (If you can only get a rectangular one, carefully fold and tear off the extra length to make it a square.)

1. Lay the napkin down with an open edge at the top and a folded corner at the bottom.

2. Lift up the first of the four layers of the napkin and roll it to the middle.

3. Turn the napkin over. Fold the left-side tip to the center.

4. Fold the right-side tip to the center.

5. Turn the napkin over. To make your pocket stronger, tape the tips to the back.

6. Stuff something in the pocket. (See how long you can keep that french fry.) Carry extra condiments with you anywhere.

Birds on a Wire

Other Foot

This is a word-association game in which you make your own word cards and pretty much make up your own rules. That leaves a lot of room for creativity! Before you start playing, read through the instructions and do a little brainstorming with your fellow players to get you in the mood for the game. Once you've done a couple of rounds, you'll be surprised how much better you get at thinking up words to play. Then you can just add them to the pile—with no set number of cards, you can keep going for miles.

How to Play

- You'll need at least three players, something to write with, and a bunch of blank cards. You could make the cards by folding and tearing regular-sized pieces of paper into smaller pieces. Try to create at least 10 cards per player, but more is better.

- When each player has his cards, the game begins. Each player writes a word or phrase on a card. There are no rules about what can be written on a card, but see the tips on the next page for the kinds of things that will make playing the game more fun.

- Each player is given five cards face-down.

- One player is chosen as the "judge." The judge collects the remaining cards (including her own five cards) and shuffles them.

- The judge chooses a card from her deck and places it face-up in the center of the group. The judge reads her card aloud for the benefit of those who might not be able to see it. (This also helps because not everyone has great handwriting).

- Each player then chooses a card from his hand that could be understood as some kind of response to the judge's card. The responding cards are given to the judge right away. (Don't spend time thinking about it).

- The judge decides which card goes best with her own card. The "best card" may somehow match her card, or perhaps finish a thought, or just sound strange in response to it. There are no rules for deciding. When the judge decides whose card is best, that player gets a "point." The player puts the judge's card in his score-pile. If the judge decides that there is no real winner, all cards from play are placed in a discard pile and no one gets a point.

- At the end of every round, all the cards that were used are placed in a discard pile to be reshuffled. All players draw a card from this pile so that they will each once again have five cards.

- Now the player seated to the left of the judge becomes the new judge.

- When everyone has played enough, the player with the most points at that moment wins.

How to Make a Good Card

- How good a card is depends on how it fits with the judge's card. What makes the game fun is having cards match up in bizarre ways. For example, "a skateboarding seal in the desert," or "a dog slobber ice-cream sundae."

- Try to come up with different kinds of things to put on your cards: very descriptive adjectives, slogans or sayings from TV or movies, times of day, strange nouns (platypus, snow cone, avalanche, fried zucchini), titles of books, habits (always wears the same socks, never washes her hair), or places (at the diner, somewhere in the suburbs of Detroit).

- This game can be really funny, but don't try to make a joke on an individual card. The fun comes from the interesting way that words or separate cards interact with each other.

- In general, stay away from using specific nouns (people, places, or things) on cards. For example, writing "a superhero" on a card could lead to funny results, but writing "Superman" usually doesn't. The more general, the better.

- Descriptive phrases are good to use too, such as "the odor of rotten fish," or "excessively jittery."

Additional Rules

- If you think of a good card you want to make while you're in the middle of the game, make it and add it to the discard pile.

- Really bad cards can be removed from the game and thrown away at any time.

- New players can join in at any time.

Bridge the Gap

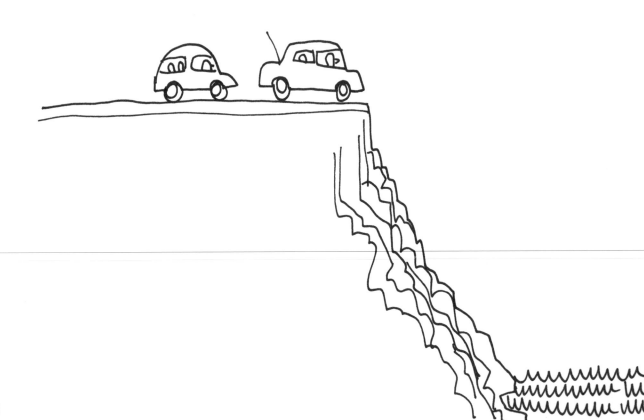

Are You Superstitious?

Traveling these days is safer than it's ever been—no need to worry about sea serpents or thieving highwaymen. But people still have a lot of superstitions about travel. Have you heard these?

Starting a Journey

- If someone says "Good luck" to you before a trip, you must answer her in some way. Otherwise, you'll have bad luck.
- It's bad luck to go back into your house immediately after you've left it. If you do have to go back in, drink a glass of water and then sit down. Or walk in and out of the house five times to confuse the evil spirits, who won't know whether you're coming or going.
- If someone lights a candle upon your departure and doesn't extinguish it until you've arrived at your destination, you'll have a safe journey.

Cemeteries

- If you pass a cemetery, hold your nose. Otherwise, the ghosts will try to enter your body through your nostrils! A variation on this superstition is that you must hold your breath or the ghosts will try to steal it from you—no breath, no life. In other words, you're dead.

- Cross your fingers and close your eyes when you go past a cemetery so the ghosts can't see you and come get you later.

Bridges

- When you're passing over a bridge in a vehicle, keep your feet off the floor. Otherwise, the water might rise and flood the bridge.
- Don't whistle on a bridge. You'll "whistle up a storm."

Overpasses

- Duck your head when you go under an overpass. If you don't, your head might get cut off!

Lucky & Unlucky Numbers

- Many hotels, especially in Asia, don't have a 13th floor because 13 is considered an unlucky number.
- Most airplanes don't have a 13th row.
- In China, four is an unlucky number, so many buildings don't have a fourth floor. It's bad luck to have

a license plate that ends in the number four. Eight is the luckiest number—the more eights you have on your license plate, the better luck you'll have.

- In Japan, the numbers 4, 9, and 13 are unlucky. Many hotels and some airlines don't use these numbers for floors or rows.
- Seventeen is an unlucky number in Italy.
- The numbers 7 and 11 are often considered good luck. Many airlines use 777 as a flight number.

Lucky Amulets

- Many believe that it's good luck to wear a religious medal when embarking on a journey.
- Wealthy travelers used to carry emeralds and garnets for good luck.
- The custom of hanging bells on horses or sleighs started as a way to keep evil spirits away from them.
- Pack a lucky coin at the bottom of your suitcase.

Traveling by Road

- Hang a lucky token on the rearview mirror or place one on the dashboard for good luck.
- If a bird poops on your car, you'll have good luck.
- If a funeral car passes you, hide your thumb.
- If a hay truck passes you, make a wish.
- If you go through a yellow light at an intersection, kiss your hand and touch the roof of the car.
- Green cars are bad luck.
- Always lift your feet and touch a screw when you go over a train track.
- If you go through a tunnel, hold your breath. If you can hold your breath the whole time through the tunnel, make a wish and it will come true.

At Sea

- Friday is an unlucky day on which to start a journey at sea.
- Never start a journey on the first Monday in April. Likewise, don't start a cruise on December 31.
- Don't enter a boat with your left foot—it's bad luck.
- "Red sky at night, sailors delight, red sky in morning, sailor take warning." In other words, don't go to sea if the morning sky is red or pinkish.
- Whistling, cutting nails, or trimming beards at sea will cause storms.
- Dolphins swimming near a ship are good luck; sharks following a ship are bad luck.
- Gold earrings were said to protect sailors from drowning. That's why you'll often see pirates wearing hoop earrings in old illustrations. In Scotland, an old law once required that sailors wear gold earrings. That way, if the sailor did drown and wash up on shore, the earring could be sold to pay for funeral expenses.

Limericks

A limerick is a five-line poem. The first two lines rhyme with the last, and the third and fourth lines rhyme with each other. Limericks are usually pretty silly, especially the last line.

Fill in the blanks to start writing your own limericks. If you want to, invent words, ignore grammar, or use words that almost rhyme, but don't quite. Sometimes using words that don't rhyme when they're supposed to can be funny.

Remember when this book was new?

Have you thought of _____?

Ask your auntie or brother

To buy you another

I'm sure that _____.

I've never _____

And never _____

Or sailed the ocean blue

But _____

And I have to say that's pretty neat.

In the fridge you'll find a bowl of _____

That mold grew on _____

_____

So kindly don't throw it away.

My dear friend, a _____ named _____

Lived in a home constructed from _____

Whenever it would thunder

I'm sure _____ would wonder:

_____?

My foolproof and perfect excuse:

First a herd of _____ got loose

Then an ocean of _____

Overwhelmed _____

I'm certain _____.

On a faraway planet we _____

The alien queen _____

We tried to amaze her

With some kind of a laser

And escaped while she _____ .

A few things you must never forget:

Wash your hands _____

Say "Please _____ "

And _____

Ah! The mysteries of etiquette.

It may seem like I have a messy room

So bad _____

_____

It's quite organized

(Though I've not seen _____ since '02).

_____ , a bully and traitor

Planned to _____ later

Rather than violence

I turned to science

And now _____ .

Listen up! I'll be explaining

A game we made up while it was raining

First _____

Then _____

Now _____ ! It's quite entertaining!

I'm tired of _____ being bland

So I'm moving to West _____

Sure, some might scoff

Some my dream might scare off

But it's better than _____ .

Low Tide

What did the tide bring in this time? Draw it on the beach.

Which Is the Real Word?

Think you have a good vocabulary? Test your skills by picking out the real English word from these lists.
Answers on page 251.

1.
A. kvard
B. kylix
C. klypct

2.
A. exquapt
B. exequy
C. exquort

3.
A. qwerty
B. qwixl
C. qwant

4.
A. lanx
B. lamnit
C. larmixx

5.
A. zooic
B. zoua
C. zoeae

6.
A. ai
B. au
C. aox

7.
A. foan
B. foin
C. fiin

8.
A. oock
B. oose
C. oolf

9.
A. judogi
B. jacoci
C. jacmiji

10.
A. xaxus
B. xebec
C. xaviv

11.
A. quoz
B. quivval
C. quock

12.
A. hwyav
B. hwyl
C. hwyck

13.
A. kyriolexy
B. kyromancy
C. kyrology

14.
A. uxuous
B. uximal
C. uxorial

15.
A. toze
B. treze
C. tuuze

16.
A. kröng
B. kreng
C. krink

17.
A. kex
B. kux
C. klax

18.
A. wvrm
B. wyxm
C. wasm

19.
A. zobuck
B. zambiz
C. zibib

20.
A. eyot
B. eyle
C. etyet

The World of Weird Words

Two places claim to have the longest place name in the world. Could it be Llanfairpwllgwyngyllgogerychwyrndrobwyll-llantysiliogogogoch, Wales? It's name, in Welsh means "The church of St. Mary in the hollow of white hazel trees near the rapid whirlpool by St. Tysilio's of the red cave."

Or is it Taumatawhakatangihangakoauauotamateapokaiwhenuakitanatahu, New Zealand, which means "The place where Tamatea, the man with the big knees, who slid, climbed, and swallowed mountains, known as 'landeater,' played his flute to his loved one"?

The longest place name in the U.S is Lake Chargoggagoggmanchauggagoggchaubunagungamaugg in Webster, Massachusetts, which means "Englishmen at Manchaug at the Fishing Place at the Boundary" in the Nipmuck language.

The longest place name in Canada is Pekwachnamaykoskwaskwaypinwanik Lake, which is in Manitoba. Its name means "where the wild trout are caught by fishing with hooks" in the local Cree language.

The old, formal Thai name for the city of Bangkok is Krungthepmahanakonbowornratanakosinmahintarayudyayamahadiloponoparatanarajthaniburiromudom-rajniwesmahasatarnamornpimarnavatarsatitsakattiyavisanukamphrasit, which means "the land of the angels, the great city of immortality, various divine gems, the great angelic land unconquerable, land of the nine noble gems, the royal city, the pleasant capital, palace of the grand royal palace, forever land of angels and reincarnated spirits, predestined and created by the highest devas."

Aiea, Hawaii is the only city name that is spelled completely with vowels.

Castaway!

Isn't this distant, completely uninhabited island lovely? It's a good thing you like it, because you and your family are going to be living here for the next two years. You'll enjoy all the perks of living in your own little paradise, but you'll have to deal with challenges as well. To survive, you need food, shelter, and protection from the elements. And the island isn't completely uninhabited: there are some wild animals living there. So pack and get ready to go. There is one rule, however: your family can only take along five things. Not five things each, but five things all together. And each person will have to agree on these things—this island is a democracy! Discuss what you'll take along. When you've all agreed on a list, write it down on the opposite page.

Some Things To Remember About the Island

There's no electricity!

There are no battery refills!

There's no refrigeration!

There are no matches!

Our Castaway Packing List

1.

2.

3.

4.

5

What Will You Need Most?

Food
Shelter
Clothing
Medical Supplies
Tools
Entertainment
Protection

Give Yourself a Hand

Trace your left hand on this page. Give yourself some cool jewelry such as rings and bracelets. Don't forget fingernails!

You're the nail stylist: come up with cool designs for these fantastic fingernails.

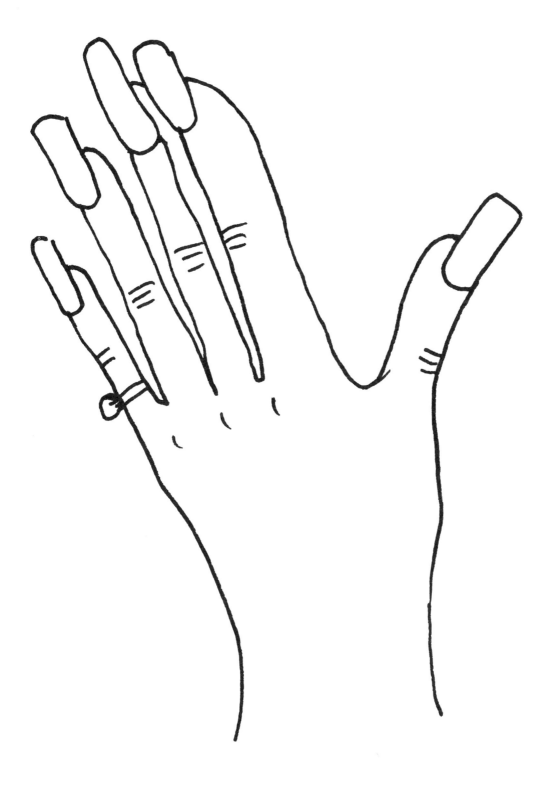

Catching Some Freshies

Wow! Six feet of fresh powder. Add skiers and snowboarders to this scene (and a snowman or two if you like). Can you make them do some cool tricks?

It's a bird! It's a plane! It's a...

Something to Smile About

Look at all these empty mouths. Fill them with teeth, braces, food, tongues, whatever.

We're Tired...

This twisting line is the answer to a maze that has yet to be drawn. We provided the solution, and it's your job to provide the maze. Make sure to include lots of dead ends.

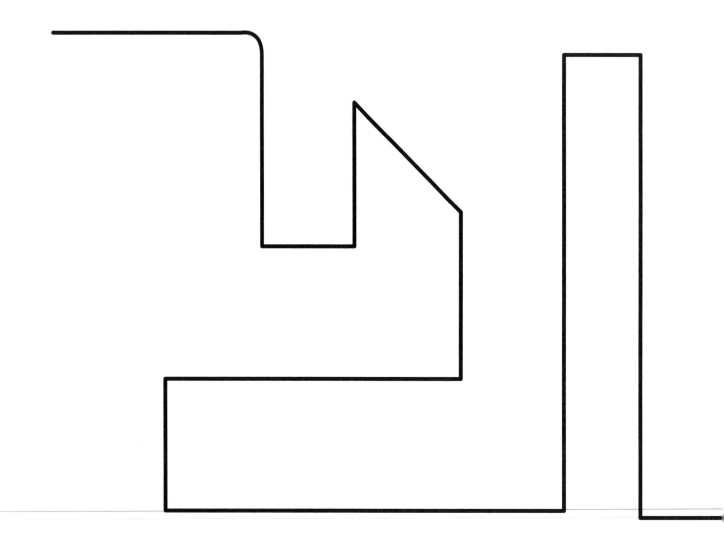

What a Long, Strange Trip It's Been

Now your trip is coming to an end. Hopefully, it was one to remember, full of interesting people, places, and things. Quick! Before you forget, write down some of the really memorable things that you experienced on your trip. Ask your fellow travelers for their memories, too.

Coolest Place We Visited

_____

_____

_____

_____

Strangest Thing I Heard Someone Say

_____

_____

_____

Weirdest Thing I Saw Somebody Do

_____

_____

_____

_____

Nicest Person I Met

_____
_____
_____
_____
_____

Weirdest Thing I Did

_____
_____
_____
_____
_____
_____

Best Thing I Ate

_____
_____
_____
_____
_____

Most Beautiful Site I Saw

_____
_____
_____

The Answer Pages

A Walk in The Woods (pages 36-37)

1. The forest represents your view of life. Is it an exciting or scary place? Peaceful or full of wild animals? Do you enjoy being there?

2. The path represents your journey through life—is it fairly straightforward, like a paved road? Or does it twist and turn?

3. The key represents knowledge. Do you pick it up or leave it there? Is it a weighty, important-looking key, or a flimsy one?

4. The obstacle in your path represents your problems. How you pass it represents how you confront your problems—do you face them head-on or go around them?

5. The size of your dream home represents the size of your dreams and goals—do you dream big or small?

6. The room represents death—is it scary to you or do you feel comfortable with it?

A Walk in the Desert (pages 38-39)

The desert represents a hardship.

Here's what each animal represents:
Lion = Pride
Monkey = Your Children
Sheep = Friendship
Cow = Basic Needs
Horse = Your Dreams

The order in which you give up the animals represents the order in which you would give up the value that each animal represents. For example, if you give up the lion first, you are a humble person; if you give it up last, you have a lot of self-importance. The animal you give up last represents the thing you value over all others.

Rebus Puzzles (pages 40-41)

1. Frankenstein
2. Ice Cube
3. Man in the moon
4. One in a million
5. Safety in Numbers
6. Go for it
7. Out in the middle of nowhere
8. Calm before the storm
9. Right behind me
10. Foreign language
11. Head over heels
12. Traveling overseas
13. Ohio
14. Big brother
15. Skating on thin ice
16. Man overboard
17. Square Dance
18. Scattered showers
19. Tennis shoes
20. Lake Ontario
21. Scrambled egg

Bumper Match (page 68)

. Earth First. We'll Log the Other Planets Later.
. You Can't Have Everything. Where Would You Put It?
. The More People I Meet, the More I Like My Dog
. This Would Be Really Funny if It Weren't Happening to Me
. A Day Without Sunshine Is Like Night
. What if the Hokey Pokey IS What It's All About?
. Honk If Anything Falls Off
. If at First You Don't Succeed, then Skydiving Is Not for You
. Caution! I Brake for Elves, Fairies, Unicorns, and Other Creatures Only I Can See
. My Other Car Is a Spaceship
. Please Hit Me So I Can Get a New Car
. Don't Follow Me—I'm Lost Too
. Minds Are Like Parachutes—They Work Best When Open
. Never Put off till Tomorrow What You Can Avoid Doing Altogether
. My Other Car Is a Broom
. If the Shoe Fits, Buy One in Every Color
. I May Be Slow But I'm Ahead of You
. I Brake for No Apparent Reason
. Good Planets Are Hard to Find

Fact or Fiction? (pages 82-83)

1. True

Although they'd have to eat more than two pounds of it, chocolate can cause vomiting, spasms, or in extreme cases, death in dogs. Some chocolate contains theobromine—although easily digested by humans, it can be lethal to dogs.

2. False

This legend is totally made up.

3. False

"Salting" was possible in the early 1990s. The saline would cause soda machines to malfunction, which would sometimes result in both money and cans of soda ejecting. Soda companies quickly caught on to this scam and changed the design of their machines.

4. False

If an eagle were to pick up a dog, it would not be able to get very far off the ground, and could not fly away with it.

5. False

There are many urban legends about "shipments from foreign places," but few of them are true.

6. False

"Gator sightings" have been reported across New York City, but it would be impossible for them to live in the cold, filthy environment of the city's sewers.

7. True

After the biggest bank heist in Japanese history (US $5.4 million was stolen), the Kobe branch of the Fukutoku Bank received a letter, presumably from the robbers. It read, "Thank you very much for the bonus. We can live off this loot for life."

8. True

In 1989, a man bought a painting at a flea market in Adamstown, Pennsylvania, because he liked the frame. When he removed the painting, the frame fell apart and between the canvas and the wooden backing, he found a copy of the Declaration of Independence from the original 500-copy print run. It later sold at auction for $2.42 million.

9. True

Sort of. Thousands report that the old Hawaiian legend of Pele, the goddess of the volcano is more than just a legend. Hawaiian tradition says that the rocks are Pele's children.

She is angered when they are taken from her, and she retaliates by cursing the thief with bad luck.

10. False

Snakes do like to burrow and hide, but they prefer to be away from humans and seek out places that will keep them warm in cold weather and vice versa.

11. False

This story is impossible because tarantulas live in holes in the ground and rarely come out to the surface.

12. True

This story happened in New York in 2005.

13. False

No one knows how many people have existed since the beginning of time. Demographers estimate the number could be anywhere from 12 to 110 billion. Because the world's population is now close to 7 billion, it's unlikely that the number will catch up with the number of dead any time soon.

14. True

Unfortunately, it is possible for this to happen.

15. False

A real rock climber started this rumor as a parable about help coming to you when you really need it.

16. True

This incident took place in 1970.

17. False

If you define "outer space" as the area beyond the Earth's atmosphere, this claim fails—no artificial structures are visible from that height.

18. True

Because pirating was illegal, pirates developed codes to talk about their activities. The "sixpence" mentioned in the rhyme let potential pirates know that they would be well paid, and the "pocket of rye" describes a type of canteen filled with alcohol—another benefit supplied to pirates. The king is said to refer to Blackbeard, the "king of the pirates," and the birds in the pie refer to the notorious pirate's crew members, nicknamed blackbirds. The rest of the rhyme alludes to luring in and attacking unsuspecting victims.

Do You Sodoku? (pages 106-109)

Example

```
2 5 4 1 3 6
6 1 3 4 5 2
3 4 5 2 6 1
1 2 6 3 4 5
5 3 1 6 2 4
4 6 2 5 1 3
```

Puzzle 1

```
4 1 3 2
2 3 4 1
1 4 2 3
3 2 1 4
```

Puzzle 2

```
1 3 2 4
4 2 3 1
3 1 4 2
2 4 1 3
```

Puzzle 3

```
3 1 6 5 2 4
5 4 2 3 1 6
6 2 4 1 3 5
1 3 5 6 4 2
2 5 1 4 6 3
4 6 3 2 5 1
```

Puzzle 4

```
5 6 4 2 1 3
2 3 1 5 6 4
3 1 6 4 2 5
4 2 5 1 3 6
6 4 2 3 5 1
1 5 3 6 4 2
```

Puzzle 5

```
1 6 2 3 5 4
4 5 3 1 2 6
6 1 4 2 3 5
2 3 5 6 4 1
5 2 1 4 6 3
3 4 6 5 1 2
```

Puzzle 6

```
4 2 6 1 3 5
1 5 3 2 6 4
6 4 1 5 2 3
5 3 2 6 4 1
3 6 5 4 1 2
2 1 4 3 5 6
```

Puzzle 7

```
5 6 4 1 3 2
1 2 3 6 5 4
3 1 2 4 6 5
6 4 5 3 2 1
4 5 6 2 1 3
2 3 1 5 4 6
```

Puzzle 8

```
2 5 6 3 4 1
4 1 3 5 2 6
1 6 4 2 5 3
5 3 2 6 1 4
6 4 5 1 3 2
3 2 1 4 6 5
```

Puzzle 9

```
4 9 3 7 6 8 1 5 2
7 2 8 5 4 1 3 9 6
5 6 1 9 2 3 7 4 8
8 1 9 4 3 6 5 2 7
3 7 2 8 1 5 4 6 9
6 4 5 2 7 9 8 1 3
2 3 4 1 9 7 6 8 5
9 5 6 3 8 4 2 7 1
1 8 7 6 5 2 9 3 4
```

Puzzle 10

```
6 5 4 1 2 9 8 7 3
9 8 3 5 7 4 1 2 6
7 1 2 6 8 3 9 4 5
4 9 5 2 3 8 7 6 1
1 6 8 4 5 7 2 3 9
2 3 7 9 1 6 4 5 8
8 7 1 3 4 5 6 9 2
5 4 9 8 6 2 3 1 7
3 2 6 7 9 1 5 8 4
```

Puzzle 11

```
1 4 6 9 2 7 8 3 5
7 3 9 5 8 6 1 4 2
8 2 5 1 4 3 6 7 9
9 1 4 7 3 5 2 8 6
2 6 8 4 1 9 7 5 3
5 7 3 2 6 8 4 9 1
4 9 7 6 5 2 3 1 8
6 8 1 3 9 4 5 2 7
3 5 2 8 7 1 9 6 4
```

Puzzle 12

```
4 7 1 6 9 5 8 2 3
3 5 8 4 2 7 6 9 1
9 6 2 3 8 1 5 4 7
6 9 3 7 5 2 4 1 8
2 4 7 1 6 8 3 5 9
1 8 5 9 3 4 2 7 6
8 1 4 5 7 6 9 3 2
5 2 9 8 1 3 7 6 4
7 3 6 2 4 9 1 8 5
```

Puzzle 13

```
9 5 2 8 7 1 6 3 4
6 1 7 5 4 3 2 8 9
8 3 4 6 9 2 1 7 5
5 7 9 3 6 8 4 1 2
2 4 1 7 5 9 3 6 8
3 8 6 1 2 4 9 5 7
4 6 3 2 8 5 7 9 1
7 2 5 9 1 6 8 4 3
1 9 8 4 3 7 5 2 6
```

Puzzle 14

```
9 1 5 8 3 2 6 7 4
4 7 8 6 9 5 3 1 2
2 6 3 1 4 7 8 5 9
8 4 6 9 5 1 7 2 3
1 2 9 3 7 4 5 6 8
3 5 7 2 6 8 4 9 1
5 3 2 4 1 6 9 8 7
7 8 4 5 2 9 1 3 6
6 9 1 7 8 3 2 4 5
```

Puzzle 15

```
7 2 1 6 3 4 8 9 5
8 9 6 7 5 2 3 1 4
4 3 5 1 8 9 2 7 6
9 1 3 2 4 6 7 5 8
5 8 2 3 7 1 6 4 9
6 4 7 5 9 8 1 3 2
1 6 9 4 2 3 5 8 7
2 5 4 8 1 7 9 6 3
3 7 8 9 6 5 4 2 1
```

Puzzle 16

```
9 4 7 2 6 8 5 3 1
2 1 3 5 7 9 6 8 4
5 6 8 1 3 4 7 9 2
8 2 4 3 5 6 9 1 7
7 9 1 8 4 2 3 5 6
3 5 6 9 1 7 4 2 8
6 3 2 4 9 1 8 7 5
1 7 5 6 8 3 2 4 9
4 8 9 7 2 5 1 6 3
```

Puzzle 17

```
2 5 8 1 4 9 6 7 3
3 1 6 8 7 5 9 2 4
7 9 4 3 6 2 5 8 1
9 6 3 2 5 1 8 4 7
1 4 5 9 8 7 2 3 6
8 2 7 4 3 6 1 9 5
4 7 9 6 1 8 3 5 2
5 8 1 7 2 3 4 6 9
6 3 2 5 9 4 7 1 8
```

Puzzle 18

```
7 4 2 9 1 6 3 8 5
9 6 8 5 3 4 7 1 2
3 5 1 2 7 8 9 4 6
6 7 5 4 2 9 1 3 8
8 2 3 7 5 1 6 9 4
1 9 4 6 8 3 5 2 7
2 8 9 1 6 5 4 7 3
5 1 7 3 4 2 8 6 9
4 3 6 8 9 7 2 5 1
```

PL8S (pages 126-127)

1. Wonderful
2. Be great.
3. I ate seafood.
4. Tomato
5. Tooth doctor (tough one, eh!?)
6. Why are you envious?
7. To the rescue.
8. Oh, to be in LA.
9. Late for a date
10. I accelerate.
11. I am the one for you.
12. Too busy for you.
13. I am for peace. Are you?
14. I see you. Are you okay?
15. I see you and I like you.
16. I be seeing you.
17. Too wise for you.

Landmark Lotto (pages 130-131)

North America

1. Devil's Tower, Wyoming
2. Gateway Arch, St. Louis
3. Golden Gate Bridge, San Francisco
4. Empire State Building, New York
5. Mount Rushmore, South Dakota

World

1. Taj Mahal, Agra, India
2. Colosseum, Rome
3. Big Ben, London
4. Sphinx, Giza, Egypt
5. Great Wall of China

Brain Jumpstart (page 170-171)

Crossing the River

1. The prison guard and the thief cross the river, and the prison guard comes back on the raft alone.
2. The prison guard takes one son over, and then comes back with the thief.
3. The father goes over with the second son, and then comes back alone.
4. The father and mother cross, and then the mother comes back alone.
5. The prison guard and the thief go back again, and the father takes the raft back alone.

6. The father and mother take the raft back, and then the mother comes back alone.
7. The mother takes the first daughter over, and then the prison guard and the thief take the raft back alone.
8. The prison guard takes the second daughter across and goes back alone.
9. The prison guard takes the thief across—now everyone is on the other side of the river!

The Night Watchman
A night watchman shouldn't sleep on the job.

How Many Fs
There are six Fs in the sentence. Most people find three of them. If you spotted four, you're above average. If you got five, or even six, you're very observant!

Hashiko (pages 174-177)

Example

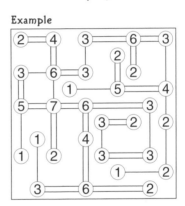

Puzzle 1

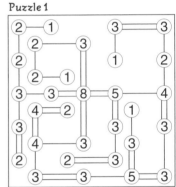

Puzzle 2

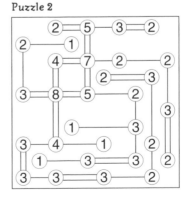

Puzzle 3

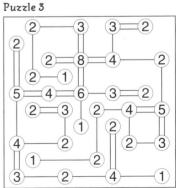

Puzzle 4

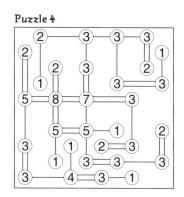

Puzzle 5

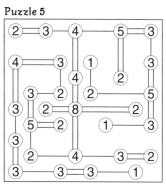

Puzzle 6

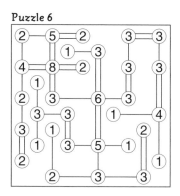

Puzzle 7

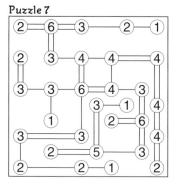

Puzzle 8

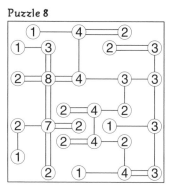

Puzzle 9

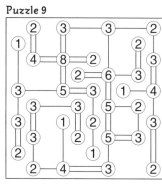

Puzzle 10

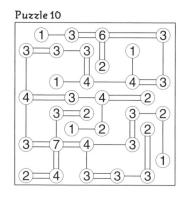

Puzzle 11

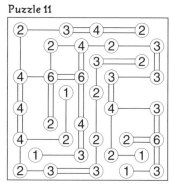

Puzzle 12

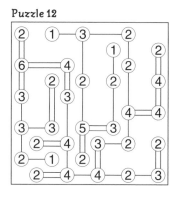

Puzzle 13

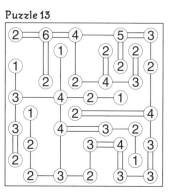

Puzzle 14

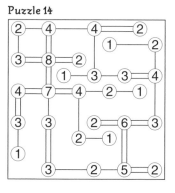

Puzzle 15

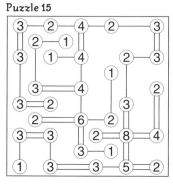

Puzzle 16

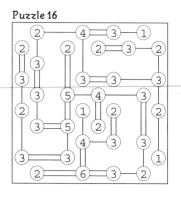

Puzzle 17

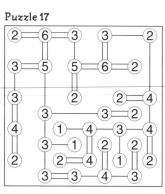

Puzzle 18

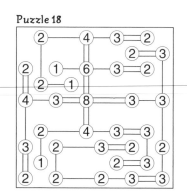

The Spooky Survival Quiz (pages 202-203)

1. A
You shouldn't really have a gun in the first place, but since a werewolf is an extenuating circumstance, you do well to have one loaded with silver bullets.

2. C
Use garlic to get to them through their sense of smell.

3. D
Once they do catch up with you, you're done for, but being fleet of foot gives you a fighting chance.

4. C
Most ghosts will respond to reason and frank discussion.

5. C
Trolls are not afraid of daisies.

6. D
A bell above the door is supposed to protect against witches—but it should be a brass one.

7. B
The giant spider's eyes would be its only vulnerable part. Having something sharp to cut your way out would be great, but you'd have to be able to move your arms first.

8. C
Knights have been using this strategy for centuries.

Which is the Real Word? (page 230)

1. B
An ancient Greek drinking cup

2. C
A funeral or burial ceremony

3. A
Of or pertaining to a keyboard layout

4. A
The plural of lance

5. C
A type of larval crab

6. A
A three-toed sloth

7. B
The tip of a sword or spear

8. B
The fluffy stuff that gathers under a bed

9. A
The clothing worn by a person practicing judo

10. B
A small, three-masted pirate ship

11. A
An absurd person

12. B
An emotional state that brings on extreme eloquence

13. A
The use of literal expressions

14. C
Of or pertaining to a wife

15. A
To comb, tease, or draw out

16. B
A whale carcass after the blubber has been removed

17. A
A dry, hollow plant stem

18. C
An outdated policy

19. C
A colorless alcoholic drink made from raisins

20. A
A small island

Your Blank Pages Start Here